THE FUTURE OF CYBER AND TELECOMMUNICATIONS SECURITY AT DHS

United States Congress House of Representatives Committee on Homeland Security, Subcommittee on Economic Security, Infrastructure Protection, and Cybersecurity

The BiblioGov Project is an effort to expand awareness of the public documents and records of the U.S. Government via print publications. In broadening the public understanding of government and its work, an enlightened democracy can grow and prosper. Ranging from historic Congressional Bills to the most recent Budget of the United States Government, the BiblioGov Project spans a wealth of government information. These works are now made available through an environmentally friendly, print-on-demand basis, using only what is necessary to meet the required demands of an interested public. We invite you to learn of the records of the U.S. Government, heightening the knowledge and debate that can lead from such publications.

Included are the following Collections:

Budget of The United States Government
Presidential Documents
United States Code
Education Reports from ERIC
GAO Reports
History of Bills
House Rules and Manual
Public and Private Laws

Code of Federal Regulations
Congressional Documents
Economic Indicators
Federal Register
Government Manuals
House Journal
Privacy act Issuances
Statutes at Large

THE FUTURE OF CYBER AND TELECOMMUNICATIONS SECURITY AT DHS

HEARING

BEFORE THE

SUBCOMMITTEE ON ECONOMIC SECURITY, INFRASTRUCTURE PROTECTION, AND CYBERSECURITY

OF THE

COMMITTEE ON HOMELAND SECURITY HOUSE OF REPRESENTATIVES

ONE HUNDRED NINTH CONGRESS

SECOND SESSION

SEPTEMBER 13, 2006

Serial No. 109–102

Printed for the use of the Committee on Homeland Security

Available via the World Wide Web: http://www.gpoaccess.gov/congress/index.html

U.S. GOVERNMENT PRINTING OFFICE

35–624 PDF   WASHINGTON : 2008

For sale by the Superintendent of Documents, U.S. Government Printing Office
Internet: bookstore.gpo.gov   Phone: toll free (866) 512–1800; DC area (202) 512–1800
Fax: (202) 512–2104   Mail: Stop IDCC, Washington, DC 20402–0001

COMMITTEE ON HOMELAND SECURITY

PETER T. KING, New York, *Chairman*

DON YOUNG, Alaska
LAMAR S. SMITH, Texas
CURT WELDON, Pennsylvania
CHRISTOPHER SHAYS, Connecticut
JOHN LINDER, Georgia
MARK E. SOUDER, Indiana
TOM DAVIS, Virginia
DANIEL E. LUNGREN, California
JIM GIBBONS, Nevada
ROB SIMMONS, Connecticut
MIKE ROGERS, Alabama
STEVAN PEARCE, New Mexico
KATHERINE HARRIS, Florida
BOBBY JINDAL, Louisiana
DAVE G. REICHERT, Washington
MICHAEL MCCAUL, Texas
CHARLIE DENT, Pennsylvania
GINNY BROWN-WAITE, Florida

BENNIE G. THOMPSON, Mississippi
LORETTA SANCHEZ, California
EDWARD J. MARKEY, Massachusetts
NORMAN D. DICKS, Washington
JANE HARMAN, California
PETER A. DeFAZIO, Oregon
NITA M. LOWEY, New York
ELEANOR HOLMES NORTON, District of
   Columbia
ZOE LOFGREN, California
SHEILA JACKSON-LEE, Texas
BILL PASCRELL, JR., New Jersey
DONNA M. CHRISTENSEN, U.S. Virgin Islands
BOB ETHERIDGE, North Carolina
JAMES R. LANGEVIN, Rhode Island
KENDRICK B. MEEK, Florida

SUBCOMMITTEE ON ECONOMIC SECURITY, INFRASTRUCTURE PROTECTION, AND CYBERSECURITY

DANIEL E. LUNGREN, California, *Chairman*

DON YOUNG, Alaska
LAMAR S. SMITH, Texas
JOHN LINDER, Georgia
MARK E. SOUDER, Indiana
MIKE ROGERS, Alabama
STEVAN PEARCE, New Mexico
KATHERINE HARRIS, Florida
BOBBY JINDAL, Louisiana
PETER T. KING, New York *(Ex Officio)*

LORETTA SANCHEZ, California
EDWARD J. MARKEY, Massachusetts
NORMAN D. DICKS, Washington
PETER A. DeFAZIO, Oregon
ZOE LOFGREN, California
SHEILA JACKSON-LEE, Texas
JAMES R. LANGEVIN, Rhode Island
BENNIE G. THOMPSON, Mississippi *(Ex Officio)*

(II)

CONTENTS

THE FUTURE OF CYBER AND TELECOMMUNICATIONS SECURITY AT DHS

Wednesday, September 13, 2006

U.S. HOUSE OF REPRESENTATIVES,
COMMITTEE ON HOMELAND SECURITY,
SUBCOMMITTEE ON ECONOMIC SECURITY, INFRASTRUCTURE
PROTECTION, AND CYBERSECURITY,
Washington, DC.

The subcommittee met, pursuant to call, at 3:21 p.m., in Room 2212, Rayburn House Office Building, Hon. Daniel Lungren [chairman of the subcommittee] presiding.

Present: Representatives Lungren, Souder, Pearce, Sanchez, Dicks, and Jackson-Lee.

Mr. LUNGREN. [Presiding.] I would like to welcome everyone this afternoon to the Subcommittee on Economic Security, Infrastructure Protection and Cybersecurity of the Homeland Security as hearing on the future of cyber and telecommunications security at Department of Homeland Security.

The security of information infrastructure has not received the emphasis that it deserves, in spite of the fact that our economy and our nation's preparedness is so dependent on this technology.

Two days ago, this country commemorated the 5-year anniversary of the worst terrorist attack on American soil. The attacks of 9/11 not only killed thousands of American citizens, but also targeted our way of life.

Those responsible have vowed to continue to attack our country and our economy.

Information and communications technology are a prime target for those intending to do us harm and a successful terrorist attack could cause immeasurable danger and damage to our everyday lives, for example, disrupt our electrical power supply or disrupt our ability to respond to emergencies.

The Department of Homeland Security has been designated the point of government contact for the critical infrastructure owners and operators within both the information technology sector and the telecommunications sector.

It is, therefore, incumbent upon the department to develop an organization that can work effectively with these two critical sectors to protect the assets under their control that benefit the entire country.

This committee has been critical of the department's priorities regarding cybersecurity and telecommunications in the past and

(1)

has called for the creation of an assistant secretary for these issues to ensure their visibility within the department.

Disappointingly, it has been over a year since the secretary announced the creation of acting secretary for cybersecurity and telecommunications, and, yet, the position has not been filled.

We are concerned the department has not been as effective as possible in ensuring the security and resiliency of our information infrastructure or its efficient reconstitution in the case of an incident of national significance.

We have been fortunate enough not to have suffered a debilitating information infrastructure incident, but we cannot rely upon good fortunate alone. We must create a strong, focused organization to ensure our cyber assets our protected and to enable us to respond effectively to a cyber incident.

Today we will hear from Undersecretary for Preparedness George Foresman, to whom the yet to be named assistant secretary will report. And we look forward to hearing your vision for the department with regard to these important issues.

We will also hear from David Powner, with the Government Accountability Office, who has reviewed the department's programs and priorities for the past several years and will present their findings and recommendations for going forward.

On our second panel, we will hear from William Pelgrin, the director of New York State's Office of Cybersecurity and Critical Infrastructure Coordination. He has experience in running a government organization task, with coordinating the protection of information infrastructure, and will provide important insight on how this can be done successfully.

Also, Mr. Paul Kurtz, executive director of the Cybersecurity Industry Alliance, will provide a private sector perspective on the department's leadership, priorities and programs.

We will also hear from Guy Copeland, the chairman of the Information Technology Sector Coordinating Council, and David Barron, the chairman of the Telecommunications Sector Coordinating Council.

Both of these gentlemen have extensive experience with managing critical information infrastructure and dealing with the department and they will provide private sector expectations and priorities for the future.

I would like to thank all the witnesses for joining us today, look forward to hearing everyone's testimony.

Before recognizing the ranking member, Ms. Sanchez, for any opening statement she may wish to make, I give everybody permission to take their coats off, because I don't know why we decided that we need to heat the place up in September in Washington, D.C. But someone has evidently thought that was a good thing.

PREPARED OPENING STATEMENT OF THE HONORABLE DANIEL LUNGREN

I would like to welcome everyone this afternoon to the Subcommittee on Economic Security, Infrastructure Protection, and Cybersecurity of the Committee on Homeland Security's hearing on the future of cyber and telecommunications security at the Department of Homeland Security.

The security of our information infrastructure has not received the emphasis that it deserves, in spite of the fact that our economy and our nation's preparedness is so dependent on this technology.

Two days ago this country commemorated the five year anniversary of the worst terrorist attack on American soil.

The attacks of 9/11 not only killed thousands of American citizens they also targeted our way of life. Those responsible have vowed to continue to attack our Country, and our economy.

Information and communications technology are a prime target for those intending to do us harm.

A successful terrorist attack could cause immeasurable damage to our everyday lives, for example, disrupt our electrical power supply or disrupt our ability to respond to emergencies.

The Department of Homeland Security has been designated the point of governmental contact for the critical infrastructure owners and operators within both the information technology sector and the telecommunications sector.

It is therefore incumbent upon DHS to develop an organization that can work effectively with these two critical sectors to protect the assets under their control that benefit the entire country.

This Committee has been critical of the Department's priorities regarding cybersecurity and telecommunications in the past and has called for the creation of an Assistant Secretary for these issues to ensure their visibility within the department.

It has been over a year since the Secretary announced the creation of an Assistant Secretary for Cyber Security and Telecommunications and yet the position has not been filled.

I am concerned that the Department has not been as effective as possible in ensuring the security and resiliency of our information infrastructure or its efficient reconstitution in the case of an incident of national significance.

We have been fortunate enough not to have suffered a debilitating information infrastructure incident, but we can not rely upon good fortune alone; we must create a strong, focused organization to ensure our cyber assets are protected and to enable us to respond effectively to a cyber incident.

Today we will hear from Under Secretary for Preparedness, George Foresman, to whom the yet to be named Assistant Secretary will report. I look forward to hearing his vision for the Department with regard to these important issues.

We will also hear from David Powner with the Government Accountability Office who has reviewed the Department's programs and priorities for the past several years and will present their findings and recommendations for going forward.

On our second panel we will hear from William Pelgrin the Director of New York State's Office of Cyber Security and Critical Infrastructure Coordination. Mr. Pelgrin has experience in running a government organization tasked with coordinating the protection of information infrastructure and will provide important insight on how this can be done successfully.

Also, Mr. Paul Kurtz, the Executive Director of the Cyber Security Industry Alliance will provide a private sector perspective on the Department's leadership, priorities and programs.

We will also hear from Guy Copeland, the chairman of the Information Technology Sector Coordinating Council and David Barron the chairman of the Telecommunications Sector Coordinating Council. Both of these gentlemen have extensive experience with managing critical information infrastructure and dealing with the Department. They will provide private sector expectations and priorities for the future.

I would like to thank all our witnesses for joining us today.

I look forward to hearing everyone's testimony, and I now recognize the Ranking Member, Ms. Sanchez, for any opening statement she may wish to make.

Ms. Sanchez?

Ms. SANCHEZ. Thank you, Mr. Chairman. Thank you for agreeing to hold this hearing. I think it is an incredibly important one.

As you know, cybersecurity is a critical issue that I believe deserves a lot more attention than this committee and others have been paying to it, and I think it also needs a lot more resources than we have devoted to it in the Department of Homeland Security.

Our whole infrastructure, when you think about business these days, relies on secure information networks, so that we can ensure that reliable operations of water systems, electrical grids, emergency response systems, Internet, everything.

In addition, for many Americans, it is really a part of their lives. This is the way we communicate. And, unfortunately, I think that the information networks that we have that we really rely on are really big areas for attack.

And, you know, we are not talking about maybe losing people, but we are talking about an economic crunch that would happen to our nation. And I am always just as concerned that the terrorists affect us economically, because then I think they will have won this issue of trying to come after our lifestyle.

So I am looking forward to hearing from our witnesses. There is a lot of issues that I am concerned with with respect to cybersecurity. I want to find out when the assistant secretary for cybersecurity and telecommunications is going to be appointed.

I think the position has been open over a year now. I also know that there are a lot of titles in this area that are still acting and I want to find out when we are going to see more permanent appointments of people, because I think that this is just one little piece, but it sends a really big message.

Do we take cybersecurity seriously? And when we have acting and empty spots, et cetera, then I think we are not devoting the resources we need. And, lastly, do we have the right resources for the department? And I look forward to discussing these.

Thank you for calling this hearing, Mr. Chairman.

Mr. LUNGREN. I thank the gentlelady for her comments.

I might say that I know the ranking member of the full committee and the chairman of the full committee wish they could be here. They are on the floor right now managing time on the bill commemorating 9/11 and the efforts of Congress thereafter.

The chair now recognizes Mr. George Foresman, the undersecretary for preparedness, to testify.

STATEMENT OF THE HONORABLE GEORGE FORESMAN, UNDERSECRETARY FOR PREPAREDNESS, DEPARTMENT OF HOMELAND SECURITY

Mr. FORESMAN. Mr. Chairman, Ranking Member Sanchez, and members of the subcommittee, thank you for the opportunity to appear today to discuss cyber and telecommunications security.

Before I begin, I would very much like to acknowledge this committee's exceptional leadership and dedication to strengthening the cybersecurity of our nation.

Mr. Chairman, I look forward to working closely with this committee to receive your guidance and to collaborate as we continue the process that we have already made.

You have my written statement and I offer that for the record.

I would like to briefly, though, highlight several points. First, there has, in fact, been much discussion about the department's ability to find and hire a qualified individual to serve as the assistant secretary for cyber and telecommunications security.

I want to be very clear. This has been and remains a top priority for the department. We are, in fact, in the final stages of a security review process for a candidate that we feel is very well qualified. We look forward to announcing the candidate with Congress very soon and I am confident that this individual will continue to build on the progress that is being made every day.

Second, today, the department is releasing its after action report from our recent government, private sector, national and international cybersecurity exercise, Cyberstorm.

This report will measurably advance refinements to operational protocols and our coordination between the public sector and the private sector.

Its lessons will not simply be documented. They will be implemented.

Third, telecommunication networks and information technology activities are both mutually dependent and interdependent. They have, in fact, converged. By the end of the year, we will complete our efforts to collocate together the U.S. computer emergency readiness team and the national coordination center for telecommunications to improve operational coordination.

This means better coordination among all levels of government and better coordination between government and the private sector during threats and actual events.

Secretary Chertoff said last week, in his speech that reflected on the 5 years since 9/11, the way to protect the critical infrastructure is to work in partnership with federal, state and local officials, and with the private sector folks who actually own the things that we are trying to protect.

This collaboration is key to our approach to protecting telecommunications and cyber infrastructure. We remain resolute in our approach that will balance the security of the nation against the economic security of the nation.

Last month, our cybersecurity experts worked quietly with their counterparts at Microsoft to address critical software vulnerability. Microsoft was competent in their partnership with DHS and quickly brought this to our attention.

While Microsoft worked over several weeks to develop a patch, our U.S. CERT was quietly and effectively monitoring Internet activity to ensure the vulnerabilities were not being exploited.

At the same time, the department was working domestically and internationally with our private sector partners and public sector partners to mitigate terrorist threats associated with the British airline plot.

These two concurrent actions are just examples of many of the day-to-day public and private sector activities taking place in the department's preparedness efforts.

Maintaining these types of collaborations remains, as you know, as it relates to cybersecurity and telecommunications security, a multi-dimensional challenge. From personal computers in homes to vast networks to control systems to the Internet, cyber and telecommunications security presents enormous challenges.

These challenges are obvious: prioritizing our work, partnering for effective collaboration, balancing security and economic considerations, and, most notably, increasing understanding.

The other witnesses today will add clarity to this points from varying perspectives. I think it is safe to say, however, there is no one that will appear before you today that does not share the belief that protecting America's cyber and telecommunications systems is as critical to national security as it is to citizen security.

I want to be clear, Mr. Chairman and members of the subcommittee. Progress is being made every day. There is more to be done.

Mr. Chairman and members of the committee, as you well know, the security of America's cyber and telecommunications systems do not lend themselves to surrounding one building with heavily armed police officers or simply mandating an action and we are safe.

Simply put, there is no magic bullet.

In closing, the success of our national cyber and telecommunications security efforts depend on unity of purpose and continuing public/private sector collaboration. This is serious business and we are serious about this business.

We look forward to continuing discussions with Congress on the wide range of policy issues that we must confront together.

Thank you, and I look forward to your questions.

[The statement of Mr. Foresman follows:]

PREPARED STATEMENT OF HON. GEORGE FORESMAN

Good morning, Mr. Chairman and Members of the Subcommittee. Thank you for inviting me to speak about cyber security and the recovery and reconstitution of critical networks in the event of a catastrophic Internet disruption.

One of the most pressing challenges facing the Department of Homeland Security is preparing for attacks on the Internet and the information networks supporting our critical infrastructure. Our vision, our philosophy, and our strategy for preventing, responding to, and recovering from cyber attacks reflect the expanding importance of communications and the information infrastructure in all aspects of our lives today. Policies that advance a safe and secure communications infrastructure rely on fostering valuable relationships between the public and private sectors, and promoting public trust and confidence. Strong policies also project stability and strength to those who wish us harm.

The key to continued success is partnering strategically with the communications and information technology sectors, end-users of Internet technologies, and other experts.

During the past several weeks our cyber security experts worked quietly with their counterparts at Microsoft to address a critical software vulnerability first identified to us by the Department of State's cyber defense team. In the interim between identification of the vulnerability and development of the solution, the Department was closely monitoring technical indicators for indications of additional exploitation of the vulnerability. Once a patch was available, the Department's U.S. Computer Emergency Readiness Team (US–CERT) coordinated an alert with Microsoft. DHS issued an alert through the National Cyber Alert System urging the public, private industry, as well as federal users to apply the security patch in order to protect their systems. Overshadowed in the news media by the successful foiling of the U.K. terror threat, this collaboration is typical of the kind of behind-the-scenes, day-to-day public-private cyber security activity that exemplifies the work being accomplished between the Department and so many of our strategic partners.

These partnerships also entail strengthening cooperation across the government institutions and, at a minimum, finding ways to cultivate support outside of the Department where expertise clearly exists. We are actively collaborating with 116 private firms. We are working closely with the private sector entities established within the National Infrastructure Protection Plan (NIPP) framework to collaborate on risk management, including the Information Technology (IT) Sector Coordinating Council (SCC) and the Telecommunications SCC. From an operational perspective, we work with the Information Technology Information Sharing and Analysis Center (IT–ISAC) and the National Coordinating Center (NCC)/Telecommunications ISAC through various information sharing mechanisms, including the US–CERT Portal. Our partners, both public and private, are involved in a number of programmatic activities that address software assurance, Internet disruption, as well as exercises such as Cyber Storm.

In addition, there are about 400 firms that are part of the Process Control Systems Forum, which was recently transferred from Science and Technology Directorate to National Cyber Security Division (NCSD) and addresses Control Systems security. There are 21 associations that we work with on a regular basis that represent hundreds of companies, including large enterprises and smaller companies. Whether public or private, these partnerships must deliver real and measurable value in light of the catastrophic damages that could occur to our national cyber assets if we do not collaborate effectively.

Finally, we must reinforce a culture of preparedness and increasingly shift from a reactive to a proactive stance. In sum, we must prepare by promoting effective security strategies that evolve as the risks evolve.

Assistant Secretary for Cyber Security and Telecommunications

Mr. Chairman, the Committee has expressed as a priority the designation of the Assistant Secretary for Cyber Security and Telecommunications, and has communicated interest in the Department's plan to fill this vacancy.

Mr. Chairman, the Department shares the Committee's view on the importance of filling the position of Assistant Secretary for Cyber Security and Telecommunications with a qualified candidate.

Given the complexity of the portfolio, we believe it is important to fill this position with a person of necessary talent and expertise who understands both policy and technology issues regarding cyber security and telecommunications and can further strengthen our national efforts.I am personally engaged in this process and, in the interim, am providing program direction to the talented men and women who are part of our NCSD and National Communications System (NCS). Because of the importance of our mission, all parties want to ensure that the individual appointed to this position possesses the right combination of skills, experience, and leadership necessary to succeed.

In the interim, I want to assure you, Mr. Chairman, that I am personally overseeing strategic management objectives associated with NCSD and specifically Internet recovery. These include, by way of example:

• Positioning the NCSD, especially the US Computer Emergency Readiness Team (US–CERT), and the NCS so these organizations are structured to be at the forefront of preventing, responding to, and recovering from massive Internet disruptions. Just as FEMA is on point for coordinating disaster response, and the Coast Guard is on point for coordinating the response to an oil spill, key experts like NCS and NCSD must be capable of coordinating our response to events that target the Internet;

• Re-aligning CS&T component entities to create a cohesive organization. The NCS and NCSD (including the US–CERT and the NCC) must more fully synchronize their activities, without a loss of either's core mission capabilities. Communications convergence, threats against the communications infrastructure, the increasing use of Voice over Internet Protocol (VOIP) for emergency communications purposes, and other influences demand that we merge the work of these entities to create new and stronger synergies and;

• Ensuring resources are sufficiently allocated to meet new needs. I am personally overseeing the development of a budget strategy that spans the next five years. This strategy is essential for shepherding CS&T priority programs into the next decade.

Information Sharing and Internet Recovery

Mr. Chairman, the Committee has communicated interest in the programs within the Department that are designed to improve information sharing regarding the recovery of the Internet

We fully recognize the challenges inherent in our preparedness responsibilities. As the President stated in the *National Strategy to Secure Cyberspace,* it is the policy of the United States to protect against "the debilitating disruption of the operation of information systems for critical infrastructures and, thereby, help to protect the people, economy, and national security of the United States." The strategy also underscores the importance of partnering with the private sector as well as State, local, and tribal governments to effectuate this policy.

On my fourth day as Undersecretary for Preparedness, I met with the Business Roundtable to discuss strategic collaboration and their Internet reconstitution study. We outlined a 120-day plan to advance our collaboration on this important work and continue to work in tandem with the Roundtable as they expand their efforts to focus on business needs and issues regarding Internet recovery and reconstitution in the coming year. The timeframes for specific actions and results will be the topic of more discussion with the Business Roundtable in the next several months. That effort supplements the work we are doing with the IT–SCC and the Telecommunications SCC under the NIPP to address Internet protection and prioritization as part of our collaborative approach to risk management in the core sectors for the Internet.

US–CERT, NCC & the NAIRG

In addition to coordinating with the Business Roundtable, our outreach specifically focuses on building relationships with private industry owners and operators of the Internet and information networks. For example, the US-Computer Emergency Readiness Team (US–CERT) continues to develop operational relationships and processes to enhance its ability to respond to an Internet disruption of national significance through its work with the IT–ISAC, and with the North American Incident Response Group (NAIRG) of industry participants. In addition, the NCC represents a fully collaborative model as the ISAC for the Telecommunications Sector, with both public and private participation in its operations.

The US–CERT has deployed several programs as part of its efforts to support cyber incident response. We expect funding in Fiscal Year 2007 to reach approximately $37 million. These funds support deployment of multiple programs, including the Einstein Program, which tracks attacks on federal information systems and warns stakeholders in near real-time. Other program areas funded as part of this total include an Internet Health Service for federal agency incident response teams, the US–CERT's 24X7 cyber incident handling center, vulnerability management, forensics education and support, and malicious code analysis.

Internet Disruption Working Group (IDWG)

The NCSD and NCS have also established an Internet Disruption Working Group (IDWG) to address the resiliency and recovery of Internet functions in the event of a major cyber incident. With public and private sector representatives, the IDWG's near-term objectives help to augment the level of information sharing among government and the private sector. The IDWG is also undertaking an information sharing assessment to better understand the information exchange landscape involving Internet incidents.

National Cyber Response Coordination Group (NCRCG)

The Business Roundtable report also underscores the role of the National Cyber Response Coordination Group (NCRCG). Established in partnership with the Department of Defense and the Department of Justice in the National Response Plan's (NRP) Cyber Annex, the NCRCG serves as the Federal government's principal interagency mechanism for coordinating the federal effort to respond to and recover from cyber incidents of national significance and includes 19 federal agencies including the Intelligence Community. The NCSD is working with industry to establish a private sector counterpart to the NCRCG, which would communicate and collaborate with the Federal government NCRCG during times of crisis.

Mr. Chairman, further detail regarding the Committee's inquiries related to the goals, resources, and timeframes for implementation associated with these programs is also provided in the Department's recent letter in response to your July 5, 2006 query.

The Role of US–CERT in Internet Recovery

Mr. Chairman, the Committee has expressed concern about the role and responsibility of the United States Computer Emergency Readiness Team with regard to Internet reconstitution.

US–CERT is the operational component of the National Cyber Security Division and represents a partnership between the Department and the public and private sectors. US–CERT is charged with protecting our nation's Internet infrastructure by coordinating defense against and response to cyber attacks. US–CERT is responsible for:

- Analyzing and reducing cyber threats and vulnerabilities;
- Disseminating cyber threat warning information; and
- Coordinating incident response activities.

As indicated above, I am personally overseeing the retooling of the US-CERT and CS&T to ensure that roles and responsibilities align with our mission with regard to Internet recovery and the NRP.

The Role of FEMA in Internet Recovery

Mr. Chairman, the Committee has communicated interest in learning about the role of the Federal Emergency Management Agency (FEMA) with regard to restoration of Internet functions in the case of a major disruption or attack.

Depending upon the nature of the disruption or attack, FEMA, under the direction of the Secretary of Homeland Security, and advised by the Assistant Secretary for Cyber Security and Telecommunications and other Department officials, may be called upon to support industry and other Federal efforts to restore connections to the Internet. FEMA's specific responsibilities under the National Response Plan through Emergency Support Function (ESF) #5—Emergency Management may entail providing logistical, communications or administrative support as they would for any other emergency or disaster that they do not have the primary lead role. However FEMA would not have the lead role for Internet restoration.

Conclusion

The National Cyber Security Division has established its mission and priority objectives, developed a strategic plan, and undertaken significant steps to implement its strategic plan across the programs outlined here. Our progress to date is tangible: we have a construct for public-private partnership; we have a track record of success in our cyber operations; we have established relationships at various levels to manage cyber incidents; we have built international communities of interest to address a global problem; and we have tested ourselves at a critical development stage and will continue to examine our internal policies, procedures, and communications paths in future exercises. We are building on each of these achievements to take further steps to address Internet recovery and reconstitution as well as to increase our overall cyber preparedness and improve our response and recovery capabilities.

In this ever-evolving environment, we know that we must always be attuned to new threats, new vulnerabilities, and new technologies. We need to be flexible enough to adjust our efforts to meet these new challenges.

I would like to thank the Subcommittee for its time today, and I appreciate this opportunity to bring further transparency to these important cyber security priorities.

Mr. LUNGREN. Thank you very much, Mr. Foresman, for your testimony.

The chair will now recognize Mr. David Powner, the director of information technology management issues at the Government Accountability Office, to testify.

And, again, the full text of your comments will be in the record, and we would ask you to summarize for 5 minutes.

STATEMENT OF DAVID POWNER, DIRECTOR, INFORMATION TECHNOLOGY MANAGEMENT ISSUES, GOVERNMENT ACCOUNTABILITY OFFICE

Mr. POWNER. Thank you, Chairman Lungren, Ranking Member Sanchez, and members of the subcommittee. We appreciate the opportunity to testify on the Department of Homeland Security's efforts associated with securing our nation's critical infrastructures from cybersecurity threats.

Recent attacks and threats have underscored the need to effectively manage and bolster cybersecurity of our nation's critical infrastructures. For example, criminal groups, foreign intelligence services, and terrorists are threats to our nation's computers and networks.

To address these threats, federal law and policy calls for critical infrastructure protection activities and establishes DHS as our nation's focal point. It also designates other agencies to coordinate with key sectors, including energy, banking and finance, and telecommunications.

This afternoon, as requested, I will summarize three key points. First, DHS has many responsibilities called for in law and policy that remain unfulfilled. Second, many challenges confront the department, including organizational stability and leadership. And, third, I will highlight our key recommendations to improve our nation's cybersecurity posture.

Expanding on each of these. Last year, we reported to you, Mr.
Chairman, that based on federal law and policy, DHS has 13 key
cybersecurity responsibilities that include developing a national
plan, enhancing public-private information sharing of cyber
threats, vulnerabilities and attacks, conducting a national cyber
threat assessment, facilitating vulnerability assessments, and coordinating incident response and recovery efforts, if, in fact, attacks
occur.

Although DHS has initiated efforts that begin to address each of
its responsibilities, the extent of progress varies and more work remains on each.

For example, its computer emergency response team, referred to
the U.S. CERT, issues warnings about vulnerabilities and coordinates responsibilities for cyber attacks. However, our nation still
lacks a national threat assessment, sector vulnerability assessments, a mature analysis of warning capability, and key recovery
plans, including a plan for recovering Internet functions.

Despite federal policy requiring DHS to develop an integrated
public-private Internet recovery plan, to date, no such plan exists.
Such a plan is important because the Internet has been targeted
and attacked and private sector companies, who own the majority
of the Internet infrastructure, deal with cyber and physical disruptions on a regular basis.

Several recent cyber attacks highlight the importance of having
robust Internet recovery plans, including a 2002 coordinated denial
of service attack that targeted all 13 Internet root servers.

DHS faces a number of challenges in building its credibility as
a stable, authoritative and capable organization that can fulfill its
cyber critical infrastructure responsibilities.

These include achieving organizational stability and authority.
Filling the assistant secretary for cyber and telecommunications
position is critical. However, leveraging this new authority will remain a challenge.

Another challenge is establishing effective partnerships and information sharing arrangements with other government entities
and the private sector.

During our most recent interviews, representatives from various
sectors told us that the level of trust is not sufficient to have productive information sharing.

In addition, DHS needs to demonstrate value, meaning that it
needs to provide useful and timely information on such items as
threats and analytical products to key stakeholders.

Regarding challenges that have impeded Internet recovery
progress, it is unclear what government entity is in charge, what
the government's role should be, and when they should get involved.

Over the last several years, we have made a series of recommendations to enhance the cybersecurity of critical infrastructures that demand immediate attention, including conducting important threat and vulnerability assessments, developing a strategic analysis and warning capability for identifying potential
threats, developing a strategy to protect infrastructure control systems, and developing recovery plans to respond to attacks, including a plan for Internet reconstitution.

In summary, Mr. Chairman, DHS has made progress in planning and coordinating efforts to enhance cybersecurity, but much more needs to be done, including conducting threat vulnerability assessments, bolstering our analytical capabilities, aggressively pursuing threat and vulnerability reduction efforts, and developing recovery plans.

Our testimony today lays out a comprehensive roadmap of key recommendations to help DHS tackle its many responsibilities.

Until DHS addresses its many challenges and more fully completes critical activities, it cannot function as the cybersecurity focal point intended in federal law and policy, resulting in increased risks that large portions of our national infrastructure will be unprepared to effectively manage cybersecurity attacks.

This concludes my statement. I would be pleased to respond to any questions.

[The statement of Mr. Powner follows:]

United States Government Accountability Office

GAO

Testimony

Before the House Committee on
Homeland Security, Subcommittee on
Economic Security, Infrastructure
Protection, and Cybersecurity

For Release on Delivery
Expected at 3 p.m. EDT
Wednesday, September 13, 2006

CRITICAL INFRASTRUCTURE PROTECTION

DHS Leadership Needed to Enhance Cybersecurity

Statement of David A. Powner
Director, Information Technology Management Issues

GAO
Accountability * Integrity * Reliability

GAO-06-1087T

Highlights of GAO-06-1087T, a testimony before the House Committee on Homeland Security, Subcommittee on Economic Security, Infrastructure Protection, and Cybersecurity.

Why GAO Did This Study

Increasing computer interconnectivity has revolutionized the way that our nation and much of the world communicate and conduct business. While the benefits have been enormous, this widespread interconnectivity also poses significant risks to our nation's computer systems and, more importantly, to the critical operations and infrastructures they support. The Homeland Security Act of 2002 and federal policy establish DHS as the focal point for coordinating activities to protect the computer systems that support our nation's critical infrastructures. GAO was asked to summarize recent reports on (1) DHS's responsibilities for cybersecurity-related critical infrastructure protection and for recovering the Internet in case of a major disruption (2) challenges facing DHS in addressing its cybersecurity responsibilities, including leadership challenges; and (3) recommendations to improve the cybersecurity of national critical infrastructures, including the Internet.

www.gao.gov/cgi-bin/getrpt?GAO-06-1087T.

To view the full product, including the scope and methodology, click on the link above. For more information, contact David Powner at (202) 512-9286 or pownerd@gao.gov.

CRITICAL INFRASTRUCTURE PROTECTION

DHS Leadership Needed To Enhance Cybersecurity

What GAO Found

In 2005 and 2006, GAO reported that DHS had initiated efforts to address its responsibilities for enhancing the cybersecurity of critical infrastructures, but that more remained to be done. Specifically, in 2005, GAO reported that DHS had initiated efforts to fulfill 13 key cybersecurity responsibilities, but it had not fully addressed any of them. For example, DHS established forums to foster information sharing among federal officials with information security responsibilities and among various law enforcement entities, but had not developed national threat and vulnerability assessments for cybersecurity. Since that time, DHS has made progress on its 13 key responsibilities—including the release of its *National Infrastructure Protection Plan*—but none have been completely addressed. Moreover, in 2006, GAO reported that DHS had begun a variety of initiatives to fulfill its responsibility to develop an integrated public/private plan for Internet recovery, but these efforts were not complete or comprehensive. For example, DHS established working groups to facilitate coordination among government and industry infrastructure officials and fostered exercises in which government and private industry could practice responding to cyber events, but many of its efforts lacked timeframes for completion and the relationships among its various initiatives were not evident.

DHS faces a number of challenges that have impeded its ability to fulfill its cybersecurity responsibilities, including establishing effective partnerships with stakeholders, demonstrating the value it can provide to private sector infrastructure owners, and reaching consensus on DHS's role in Internet recovery and on when the department should get involved in responding to an Internet disruption. DHS faces a particular challenge in attaining the organizational stability and leadership it needs to gain the trust of other stakeholders in the cybersecurity world—including other government agencies as well as the private sector. In May 2005, we reported that multiple senior DHS cybersecurity officials had recently left the department. In July 2005, DHS undertook a reorganization which established the position of the Assistant Secretary of Cyber Security and Telecommunications—in part to raise the visibility of cybersecurity issues in the department. However, over a year later, this position remains vacant.

To strengthen DHS's ability to implement its cybersecurity responsibilities and to resolve underlying challenges, GAO has made about 25 recommendations over the last several years. These recommendations focus on the need to (1) conduct threat and vulnerability assessments, (2) develop a strategic analysis and warning capability for identifying potential cyber attacks, (3) protect infrastructure control systems, (4) enhance public/private information sharing, and (5) facilitate recovery planning, including recovery of the Internet in case of a major disruption. These recommendations provide a high-level road map for DHS to use to help improve our nation's cybersecurity posture. Until they are addressed, DHS will have difficulty achieving results as the federal cybersecurity focal point.

Mr. Chairman and Members of the Subcommittee:

Thank you for the opportunity to join in today's hearing on the need for leadership in protecting our nation's critical infrastructures from cybersecurity threats. Increasing computer interconnectivity—most notably growth in the use of the Internet—has revolutionized the way that our government, our nation, and much of the world communicate and conduct business. While the benefits have been enormous, this widespread interconnectivity also poses significant risks to the government's and our nation's computer systems and, more importantly, to the critical operations and infrastructures they support.

Federal regulation establishes the Department of Homeland Security (DHS) as the focal point for the security of cyberspace—including analysis and warning, information sharing, vulnerability reduction, and recovery efforts for public and private critical infrastructure information systems.[1] Additionally, federal policy recognizes the need to be prepared for the possibility of debilitating Internet disruptions and—because the vast majority of the Internet's infrastructure is owned and operated by the private sector—tasks DHS with developing an integrated public/private plan for Internet recovery.[2]

As requested, our testimony will summarize our recent work on (1) DHS's responsibilities for cybersecurity-related critical infrastructure protection and, more specifically, its responsibilities for recovering the Internet in case of a major disruption, (2) challenges facing DHS in addressing its cybersecurity responsibilities, including leadership challenges, and (3) recommendations to improve the cybersecurity of national critical infrastructures, including the Internet. In preparing for this testimony, we relied on our previous reports on the challenges faced by DHS in fulfilling its cybersecurity responsibilities and in

---

[1] Homeland Security Presidential Directive 7: Critical Infrastructure Identification, Prioritization, and Protection (Dec. 17, 2003).

[2] The White House, *National Strategy to Secure Cyberspace* (Washington, D.C.: February 2003).

facilitating the recovery of the Internet in case of a major
disruption.[3] These reports contain detailed overviews of the scope
and methodology we used. All of the work on which this testimony
is based was performed in accordance with generally accepted
government auditing standards.

Results in Brief

As the focal point for critical infrastructure protection, DHS has
many cybersecurity-related responsibilities that are called for in law
and policy. In 2005 and 2006, we reported that DHS had initiated
efforts to address these responsibilities, but that more remained to
be done.[4] Specifically, in 2005, we reported that DHS had initiated
efforts to fulfill 13 key cybersecurity responsibilities, but it had not
fully addressed any of them. For example, DHS established forums
to foster information sharing among federal officials with
information security responsibilities and among various law
enforcement entities, but had not developed national threat and
vulnerability assessments for cybersecurity. Since that time, DHS
has made progress on its responsibilities—including the release of
its National Infrastructure Protection Plan—but none has been
completely addressed. Moreover, in 2006, we reported that DHS had
begun a variety of initiatives to fulfill its responsibility to develop an
integrated public/private plan for Internet recovery, but that these
efforts were not complete or comprehensive. For example, DHS had
established working groups to facilitate coordination among
government and industry infrastructure officials and fostered
exercises in which government and private industry could practice
responding to cyber events, but many of its efforts lacked

[3]GAO, *Critical Infrastructure Protection: Department of Homeland Security Faces
Challenges in Fulfilling Cybersecurity Responsibilities*, GAO-05-434 (Washington, D.C.: May
26, 2005); *Critical Infrastructure Protection: Challenges in Addressing Cybersecurity*, GAO-
05-827T (Washington, D.C.: July 19, 2005); *Internet Infrastructure: DHS Faces Challenges
in Developing a Joint Public/Private Recovery Plan*, GAO-06-672 (Washington, D.C.: June
16, 2006); *Internet Infrastructure: Challenges in Developing a Public/Private Recovery Plan*,
GAO-06-863T (Washington, D.C.: July 28, 2006).

[4]GAO-05-434 and GAO-06-672.

17

timeframes for completion and the relationships among its various initiatives are not evident.

DHS faces a number of challenges that have impeded its ability to fulfill its cybersecurity responsibilities, including establishing effective partnerships with stakeholders, achieving two-way information sharing with stakeholders, demonstrating the value it can provide to private sector infrastructure owners, and reaching consensus on DHS's role in Internet recovery and on when the department should get involved in responding to an Internet disruption. DHS faces a particular challenge in attaining the organizational stability and leadership it needs to gain the trust of other stakeholders in the cybersecurity world—including other government agencies as well as the private sector. In May 2005, we reported that multiple senior DHS cybersecurity officials had recently left the department. In July 2005, DHS undertook a reorganization which established the position of the Assistant Secretary of Cyber Security and Telecommunications—in part to raise the visibility of cybersecurity issues in the department. However, over a year later, this position remains vacant. While DHS stated that the lack of a permanent assistant secretary has not hampered its efforts related to protecting critical infrastructures, several private-sector representatives stated that DHS's lack of leadership in this area has limited its progress.

To strengthen DHS's ability to implement its cybersecurity responsibilities and to resolve underlying challenges, GAO has made about 25 recommendations over the last several years. These recommendations focus on the need to (1) conduct important threat and vulnerability assessments, (2) develop a strategic analysis and warning capability for identifying potential cyber attacks, (3) protect infrastructure control systems, (4) enhance public/private information sharing, and (5) facilitate recovery planning, including recovery of the Internet in case of a major disruption. Together, the recommendations provide a high-level road map for DHS to use in working to improve our nation's cybersecurity posture. Until it addresses these recommendations, DHS will have difficulty achieving results in its role as the federal focal point for the cybersecurity of critical infrastructures—including the Internet.

18

Background

The same speed and accessibility that create the enormous benefits of the computer age can, if not properly controlled, allow individuals and organizations to inexpensively eavesdrop on or interfere with computer operations from remote locations for mischievous or malicious purposes, including fraud or sabotage. In recent years, the sophistication and effectiveness of cyberattacks have steadily advanced. These attacks often take advantage of flaws in software code, circumvent signature-based tools[5] that commonly identify and prevent known threats, and use social engineering techniques designed to trick the unsuspecting user into divulging sensitive information or propagating attacks.

Government officials are increasingly concerned about attacks from individuals and groups with malicious intent, such as crime, terrorism, foreign intelligence-gathering, and acts of war. As greater amounts of money are transferred through computer systems, as more sensitive economic and commercial information is exchanged electronically, and as the nation's defense and intelligence communities increasingly rely on commercially available information technology, the likelihood increases that information attacks will threaten vital national interests.

Recent attacks and threats have further underscored the need to bolster the cybersecurity of our government's and our nation's computer systems and, more importantly, of the critical operations and infrastructures they support. Recent examples of attacks include the following:

- In March 2005, security consultants within the electric industry reported that hackers were targeting the U.S. electric power grid and had gained access to U.S. utilities' electronic control systems. Computer security specialists reported that, in a few cases, these intrusions had "caused an impact." While officials

---

[5]Signature-based tools compare files or packets to a list of "signatures"—patterns of specific files or packets that have been identified as threats.

stated that hackers had not caused serious damage to the systems that feed the nation's power grid, the constant threat of intrusion has heightened concerns that electric companies may not have adequately fortified their defenses against a potential catastrophic strike.

- In January 2005, a major university reported that a hacker had broken into a database containing 32,000 student and employee social security numbers, potentially compromising their identities and finances. In similar incidents during 2003 and 2004, it was reported that hackers had attacked the systems of other universities, exposing the personal information of over 1.8 million people.

- In June 2003, the U.S. government issued a warning concerning a virus that specifically targeted financial institutions. Experts said the BugBear.b virus was programmed to determine whether a victim had used an e-mail address for any of the roughly 1,300 financial institutions listed in the virus's code. If a match were found, the software attempted to collect and document user input by logging keystrokes and then provided this information to a hacker, who could use it in attempts to break into the banks' networks.

- In January 2003, the Slammer worm infected more than 90 percent of vulnerable computers worldwide within 10 minutes of its release on the Internet by exploiting a known vulnerability for which a patch had been available for 6 months.[6] Slammer caused network outages, canceled airline flights, and automated teller machine failures. In addition, the Nuclear Regulatory Commission confirmed that the Slammer worm had infected a private computer network at a nuclear power plant, disabling a safety monitoring system for nearly 5 hours and causing the plant's process computer to fail. The worm reportedly also affected communication on the control networks of at least five utilities by propagating so quickly that control system traffic was

---

[6] GAO-06-672.

blocked. Cost estimates on the impact of the work range from $1.05 billion to $1.25 billion.

In May 2005, we reported that federal agencies were facing a set of emerging cybersecurity threats as a result of increasingly sophisticated methods of attack and the blending of once distinct types of attack into more complex and damaging forms.[7] Examples of these threats include spam (unsolicited commercial e-mail), phishing (fraudulent messages used to obtain personal or sensitive data), and spyware (software that monitors user activity without the user's knowledge or consent). Spam consumes significant resources and is used as a delivery mechanism for other types of cyberattacks; phishing can lead to identity theft, loss of sensitive information, and reduced trust and use of electronic government services; and spyware can capture and release sensitive data, make unauthorized changes, and decrease system performance. These attacks are also becoming increasingly automated with the use of botnets—compromised computers that can be remotely controlled by attackers to automatically launch attacks. Bots (short for robots) have become a key automation tool that is used to speed the infection of vulnerable systems.

Federal law and regulation call for critical infrastructure protection activities that are intended to enhance the cyber and physical security of both the public and private infrastructures that are essential to national security, national economic security, and national public health and safety.[8] Federal regulation also establishes DHS as the focal point for the security of cyberspace—including analysis, warning, information sharing, vulnerability reduction, mitigation, and recovery efforts for public and private critical infrastructure information systems. To accomplish this mission, DHS is to work with other federal agencies, state and local governments, and the private sector. Federal policy further recognizes the need to prepare for debilitating Internet disruptions and—because the vast majority of the Internet infrastructure is

---

[7]GAO, *Information Security: Emerging Cybersecurity Issues Threaten Federal Information Systems*, GAO-05-231 (Washington, D.C.: May 13, 2005).

[8]The Homeland Security Act of 2002 and the Homeland Security Presidential Directive 7.

owned and operated by the private sector—tasks the DHS with developing an integrated public/private plan for Internet recovery.[9]

Prior Reports Identified DHS's Efforts to Fulfill Cybersecurity Responsibilities

As the focal point for critical infrastructure protection, the Department of Homeland Security (DHS) has many cybersecurity-related roles and responsibilities that are called for in law and policy. These responsibilities include developing plans, building partnerships, and improving information sharing, as well as implementing activities related to the five priorities in the *National Strategy to Secure Cyberspace*. These priorities are (1) developing and enhancing national cyber analysis and warning, (2) reducing cyberspace threats and vulnerabilities, (3) promoting awareness of and training in security issues, (4) securing governments' cyberspace, and (5) strengthening national security and international cyberspace security cooperation. See table 1 for a list of DHS's 13 key cybersecurity responsibilities. These responsibilities are described in more detail in appendix I. To fulfill its cybersecurity role, in June 2003, DHS established the National Cyber Security Division to take the lead in addressing the cybersecurity of critical infrastructures.

[9]The White House, *National Strategy to Secure Cyberspace* (Washington, D.C.: February 2003).

22

Table 1: DHS's Key Cybersecurity Responsibilities

• Develop a comprehensive national plan for critical infrastructure protection, including cybersecurity.	• Support efforts to reduce cyber threats and vulnerabilities.
• Develop partnerships and coordinate with other federal agencies, state and local governments, and the private sector.	• Promote and support research and development efforts to strengthen cyberspace security.
• Improve and enhance public/private information sharing involving cyber attacks, threats, and vulnerabilities.	• Promote awareness and outreach.
	• Foster training and certification.
• Develop and enhance national cyber analysis and warning capabilities.	• Enhance federal, state, and local government cybersecurity.
• Provide and coordinate incident response and recovery planning efforts.	• Strengthen international cyberspace security.
• Identify and assess cyber threats and vulnerabilities.	• Integrate cybersecurity with national security.

Source: GAO analysis of the Homeland Security Act of 2002, the Homeland Security Presidential Directive-7, and the *National Strategy to Secure Cyberspace*.

In our 2005 report and testimony, we noted that while DHS initiated multiple efforts to fulfill its responsibilities, it had not fully addressed any of the 13 responsibilities, and much work remained to fulfill them.[18] For example, the department established the United States Computer Emergency Readiness Team as a public/private partnership to make cybersecurity a coordinated national effort, and it established forums to build greater trust and information sharing among federal officials with information security responsibilities and law enforcement entities. However, DHS had not yet developed national cyber threat and vulnerability assessments or government/industry contingency recovery plans for cybersecurity. Since that report was issued, DHS has made progress on its responsibilities, but none have been completely addressed. For example, in June 2006, the agency released the National Infrastructure Protection Plan; however, supplemental sector-specific plans have not yet been finalized. Further, DHS reported that it has expanded the use of a situational awareness tool that supports cyber analysis and warning from one to seven federal

[18]GAO-05-434 and GAO-05-827T.

agencies. However, this does not yet comprise a national analysis and warning capability.

In our 2006 report and testimony, we focused particularly on one of DHS's key cybersecurity responsibilities—facilitating Internet recovery.[11] We reported that DHS had begun a variety of initiatives to fulfill its responsibility for developing an integrated public/private plan for Internet recovery, but that these efforts were not comprehensive or complete. For example, DHS had developed high-level plans for infrastructure protection and incident response; however, the components of these plans that address the Internet infrastructure were not complete. Further, several representatives of private-sector firms supporting the Internet infrastructure expressed concerns about the plans, noting that the plans would be difficult to execute in times of crisis. The department had also started a variety of initiatives to improve the nation's ability to recover from Internet disruptions, including establishing working groups to facilitate coordination and exercises in which government and private industry practice responding to cyber events. However, progress to date on these initiatives had been limited, and other initiatives lacked time frames for completion. Also, the relationships among these initiatives were not evident. As a result, we reported that the government was not yet adequately prepared to effectively coordinate public/private plans for recovering from a major Internet disruption. A private-sector organization subsequently reported that our nation was unprepared to reconstitute the Internet after a massive disruption, noting that there were significant gaps in government response plans and that the responsibilities of the multiple organizations that would plan a role in recovery were unclear.[12]

---

[11]GAO-06-672 and GAO-06-863T.

[12]*Business Roundtable, Essential Steps to Strengthen America's Cyber Terrorism Preparedness* (Washington, D.C.: June 2006).

DHS Faces Many Challenges; Organizational Stability and Leadership Are Keys to Success

DHS faces numerous challenges in fulfilling its cybersecurity-related CIP responsibilities. Key challenges in fulfilling DHS's broad responsibilities include increasing awareness about cybersecurity roles and capabilities, establishing effective partnerships with stakeholders, achieving two-way information sharing with these stakeholders, and demonstrating the value it can provide to private sector infrastructure owners. Key challenges to establishing a plan for recovering from Internet disruptions include addressing innate characteristics of the Internet that make planning for and responding to disruptions difficult, achieving consensus on DHS's role[13] and on when the department should get involved in responding to a disruption, addressing legal issues affecting DHS's ability to provide assistance to restore Internet service, and overcoming reluctance of many in the private sector to share information on Internet disruptions with DHS. Further, the department faces a particular challenge in attaining the organizational stability and leadership it needs to gain the trust of other stakeholders in the cybersecurity world—including other government agencies as well as the private sector.

In May 2005, we reported that multiple senior DHS cybersecurity officials had recently left the department.[14] These officials included the NCSD Director, the Deputy Director responsible for Outreach and Awareness, the Director of the US-CERT Control Systems Security Center, the Under Secretary for the Information Analysis and Infrastructure Protection Directorate and the Assistant Secretary responsible for the Information Protection Office.

---

[13]While some private sector officials we spoke to stated that the government did not have a direct recovery role, others identified a variety of potential roles including providing information on specific threats, providing security and disaster relief during a crisis, funding backup communication infrastructures, driving improved Internet security through requirements for the government's own procurements, and providing logistical assistance, such as fuel, power, and security to Internet infrastructure operators during a crisis.

[14]GAO-05-434.

Infrastructure sector officials stated that the lack of stable leadership has diminished NCSD's ability to maintain trusted relationships with its infrastructure partners and has hindered its ability to adequately plan and execute activities. According to one private-sector representative, the importance of organizational stability in fostering strong partnerships cannot be over emphasized.

In July 2005, DHS underwent a reorganization which elevated responsibility for cybersecurity to an assistant secretary position. NCSD and the National Communication System were placed in the Preparedness Directorate under a new position, called the Assistant Secretary of Cyber Security and Telecommunications—in part to raise the visibility of cybersecurity issues in the department. However, over a year later, this position remains vacant. While DHS stated that the lack of a permanent assistant secretary has not hampered its efforts related to protecting critical infrastructure, several private-sector representatives stated that DHS's lack of leadership in this area has limited progress. Specifically, these representatives stated that filling key leadership positions would enhance DHS's visibility to the Internet industry and would potentially improve its reputation.

Implementation of GAO's Recommendations Should Enhance DHS's Ability to Fulfill Cybersecurity Responsibilities and Address Challenges

To strengthen DHS's ability to implement its cybersecurity responsibilities and to resolve underlying challenges, GAO has made about 25 recommendations over the last several years. These recommendations focus on the need to (1) conduct threat and vulnerability assessments, (2) develop a strategic analysis and warning capability for identifying potential cyber attacks, (3) protect infrastructure control systems, (4) enhance public/private information sharing, and (5) facilitate recovery planning, including recovery of the Internet in case of a major disruption. These recommendations are summarized below and key recommendations that have not yet been fully implemented are listed in appendix 2. Together, the recommendations provide a high-level roadmap for DHS to use to improve our nation's cybersecurity posture. Until it addresses these recommendations, DHS will have difficulty achieving results in its role as a federal focal point for cybersecurity of critical infrastructures.

Threat and Vulnerability Assessments: In May 2005, we reported that while DHS had made progress in planning and coordinating efforts to enhance cybersecurity, much more work remained to be done for the department to fulfill its basic responsibilities—including conducting important threat and vulnerability assessments.[15] Specifically, we noted that DHS had participated in national efforts to identify and assess cyber threats and had begun to take steps to facilitate sector-specific vulnerability assessments, but that it had not completed a national cyber threat assessment, sector-specific vulnerability assessments, or the identification of cross-sector interdependencies that are called for in the cyberspace strategy. We made recommendations to strengthen the department's ability to implement key cybersecurity responsibilities by prioritizing and completing critical activities and resolving underlying challenges. DHS concurred with our recommendation to engage stakeholders in prioritizing its key cybersecurity responsibilities, including performing a national cyber threat assessment and facilitating sector cyber vulnerability assessments. However, these efforts are not yet complete.

Strategic Analysis and Warnings: In 2001, we reported on the analysis and warnings efforts within DHS's predecessor, the National Infrastructure Protection Center, and we identified several challenges that were impeding the development of an effective strategic analysis and warning capability.[16] We reported that a generally accepted methodology for analyzing strategic cyber-based threats did not exist. Specifically, there was no standard terminology, no standard set of factors to consider, and no established thresholds for determining the sophistication of attack techniques. We also reported that the Center did not have the industry-specific data on factors such as critical systems components, known vulnerabilities, and interdependencies.

---

[15]GAO-05-434.

[16]GAO, *Critical Infrastructure Protection: Significant Challenges in Developing National Capabilities*, GAO-01-323 (Washington, D.C.: Apr. 25, 2001).

We therefore recommended that the responsible executive-branch officials and agencies establish a capability for strategic analysis of computer-based threats, including developing a methodology, acquiring expertise, and obtaining infrastructure data.

More recently, in 2005, we reported that DHS had established various initiatives to enhance its analytical capabilities, including intelligence-sharing through the US CERT and situational awareness tools through the US CERT Einstein program at selected federal agencies. However, we noted that DHS was still facing the same challenges in developing strategic analysis and warning capabilities and that our original recommendations had not been fully implemented.

Control Systems: In March 2004, we reported that several factors—including the adoption of standardized technologies with known vulnerabilities and the increased connectivity of control systems to other systems—had contributed to an escalation of the risk of cyber-attacks against control systems.[17] We recommended that DHS develop and implement a strategy for coordinating with the private sector and with other government agencies to improve control system security, including an approach for coordinating the various ongoing efforts to secure control systems. DHS concurred with our recommendation and, in December 2004, issued a high-level national strategy for control systems security. This strategy includes, among other things, goals to create a capability to respond to attacks on control systems and to mitigate vulnerabilities, bridge industry and government efforts, and develop control systems security awareness. However, the strategy does not yet include underlying details and milestones for completing activities. In 2007, we plan to evaluate federal efforts to enhance the protection of critical control systems.

Information Sharing: Over the years, we have issued a series of reports, summarized below, on efforts to improve information sharing in support of critical infrastructure protection. Further,

---

[17]GAO, *Critical Infrastructure Protection: Challenges and Efforts to Secure Control Systems*, GAO-04-354 (Washington, D.C.: Mar. 15, 2004).

because of the importance of this topic, in January 2005, we designated establishing appropriate and effective information-sharing mechanisms to improve homeland security as a new high-risk area in our report on federal programs and operations at risk.[18] We reported that the ability to share security-related information can unify the efforts of federal, state, and local government agencies and the private sector in preventing or minimizing terrorist attacks.

In July 2004, we recommended actions to improve the effectiveness of DHS's information-sharing efforts.[19] We recommended that officials within the Information Analysis and Infrastructure Protection Directorate (1) proceed with and establish milestones for developing an information-sharing plan and (2) develop appropriate DHS policies and procedures for interacting with ISACs, sector coordinators (groups or individuals designated to represent their respective infrastructure sectors' CIP activities), and sector-specific agencies and for coordination and information sharing within the Information Analysis and Infrastructure Protection Directorate and other DHS components. DHS stated that the report generally provided an accurate analysis and planned actions to address these recommendations. However, as of today, the recommendations have not yet been implemented.

More recently, in March 2006, we reported that more than 4 years after September 11, the nation still lacked governmentwide policies and processes to help agencies integrate a myriad of ongoing efforts to improve the sharing of terrorism-related information that is critical to protecting our homeland.[20] Responsibility for creating these policies and processes now lies with the Director of National Intelligence—and should include a cybersecurity focus. We made several recommendations to the Director of National Intelligence to strengthen information sharing efforts.

[18]GAO, *High-Risk Series: An Update*, GAO-05-207 (Washington, D.C.: January 2005).

[19]GAO, *Critical Infrastructure Protection: Improving Information Sharing with Infrastructure Sectors*, GAO-04-780 (Washington, D.C.: July 9, 2004).

[20]GAO, *Information Sharing: The Federal Government Needs to Establish Policies and Processes for Sharing Terrorism-Related and Sensitive but Unclassified Information*, GAO-06-385 (Washington, D.C.: March 17, 2006).

Most recently, in April 2006, we reported on DHS's efforts to
implement the Critical Infrastructure Information Act of 2002, which
was enacted to encourage nonfederal entities to voluntarily share
critical infrastructure information and established protections for
it.[21] DHS has initiated several actions, including issuing interim
operating procedures[22] and creating a program office to administer
the critical infrastructure protection program called for by the
Critical Infrastructure Information Act. The program office has also
begun to accept and safeguard critical infrastructure information
submitted voluntarily by infrastructure owners and is sharing it with
other DHS entities and, on a limited basis, with other government
entities. For example, as of January 2006, the program office had
received about 290 submissions of critical infrastructure
information from various sectors. However, DHS faces challenges
that impede the private sector's willingness to share sensitive
information, including defining specific government needs for
critical infrastructure information, determining how the information
will be used, assuring the private sector that the information will be
protected and who will be authorized to have access to the
information, and demonstrating to critical infrastructure owners the
benefits of sharing the information. We recommended that DHS
better define its own and other federal agencies' critical
infrastructure information needs and explain how it and the other
agencies will use the information they receive from the private
sector. We also recommended that DHS establish a specific deadline
for issuing its final operating procedures. DHS concurred with our
findings and recommendations and has made progress in selected
areas. Specifically, on September 1, 2006, DHS released its final
operating procedures.[23]

---

[21]GAO, *Information Sharing: DHS Should Take Steps to Encourage More Widespread Use
of Its Program to Protect and Share Critical Infrastructure Information*, GAO-06-383
(Washington, D.C.: April 17, 2006).

[22]On February 20, 2004, DHS issued *Procedures for Handling Critical Infrastructure
Information: Interim Rule* (69 FR 8074) that, among other things, included mechanisms
specified in law, established authorities regarding the sharing of information, and stated
that DHS would consider issuing supplemental regulations.

[23]Department of *Homeland Security, Procedures* for Handling Critical Infrastructure
Information; Final Rule (71 FR 52262) (Sept. 1, 2006).

Recovery Planning: In May 2005, we reported that while DHS had made progress in planning and coordinating efforts to enhance cybersecurity, much more work remained to be done to fulfill its responsibilities—including facilitating government and government/industry cybersecurity recovery plans.[24] More recently, in June 2006, we reported that DHS had begun a variety of initiatives to fulfill its responsibility for developing an integrated public/private plan for Internet recovery, but that these efforts were not complete or comprehensive.[25] Further, we reported that DHS faced key challenges in establishing a plan for recovering from Internet disruptions, including obtaining consensus on its role and on when the department should get involved in responding to a disruption, overcoming the reluctance of many in the private sector to share information on Internet disruptions, addressing leadership uncertainties within the department. We made recommendations to strengthen the department's ability to help recover from Internet disruptions. DHS concurred with our recommendations and identified plans to begin addressing them.

We also reported that the federal laws and regulations that address critical infrastructure protection, disaster recovery, and the telecommunications infrastructure provide broad guidance that applies to the Internet, but it is not clear how useful these authorities would be in helping to recover from a major Internet disruption. Specifically, key legislation on critical infrastructure protection does not address roles and responsibilities in the event of an Internet disruption. Other laws and regulations governing disaster response and emergency communications have never been used for Internet recovery. We suggested that Congress consider clarifying the legal framework guiding Internet recovery.

In summary, while DHS has initiatives underway to fulfill its many cybersecurity responsibilities, major tasks remain to be done. These include assessing and reducing cyber threats and vulnerabilities and

[24]GAO-05-434.

[25]GAO-06-672.

coordinating incident response and recovery planning efforts. In fulfilling its cybersecurity responsibilities, DHS has many challenges to overcome, several of which will be difficult without effective leadership. Effective leadership is essential in order to fulfill key government responsibilities and to partner and build credibility with the private sector. Addressing this leadership void starts with DHS naming its Assistant Secretary of Cyber Security and Telecommunications. Once that position is filled, our recommendations in the areas of threat and vulnerability analysis, analysis and warning, control systems protection, information sharing, and recovery planning can help prioritize efforts to secure our nation's public and private infrastructures.

Mr. Chairman, this concludes my statement. I would be happy to answer any questions at this time.

If you have any questions on matters discussed in this testimony, please contact us at (202) 512-9286 or by e-mail at pownerd@gao.gov. Other key contributors to this report include Colleen Phillips (Assistant Director), Vijay D'Souza, Michael Gilmore, Barbarol James, and Teresa Neven.

Appendix I: Thirteen DHS Cybersecurity Responsibilities

Critical infrastructure protection responsibilities with a cyber element	Description
Develop a national plan for critical infrastructure protection that includes cybersecurity.	Developing a comprehensive national plan for securing the key resources and critical infrastructure of the United States, including information technology and telecommunications systems (including satellites) and the physical and technological assets that support such systems. This plan is to outline national strategies, activities, and milestones for protecting critical infrastructures.
Develop partnerships and coordinate with other federal agencies, state and local governments, and the private sector.	Fostering and developing public/private partnerships with and among other federal agencies, state and local governments, the private sector, and others. DHS is to serve as the "focal point for the security of cyberspace."
Improve and enhance public/private information sharing involving cyber attacks, threats, and vulnerabilities.	Improving and enhancing information sharing with and among other federal agencies, state and local governments, the private sector, and others through improved partnerships and collaboration, including encouraging information sharing and analysis mechanisms. DHS is to improve sharing of information on cyber attacks, threats, and vulnerabilities.
Responsibilities related to the cyberspace strategy's five priorities	
Develop and enhance national cyber analysis and warning capabilities.	Providing cyber analysis and warnings, enhancing analytical capabilities, and developing a national indications and warnings architecture to identify precursors to attacks.
Provide and coordinate incident response and recovery planning efforts.	Providing crisis management in response to threats to or attacks on critical information systems. This entails coordinating efforts for incident response, recovery planning, exercising cybersecurity continuity plans for federal systems, planning for recovery of Internet functions, and assisting infrastructure stakeholders with cyber-related emergency recovery plans.
Identify and assess cyber threats and vulnerabilities.	Leading efforts by the public and private sector to conduct a national cyber threat assessment, to conduct or facilitate vulnerability assessments of sectors, and to identify cross-sector interdependencies.
Support efforts to reduce cyber threats and vulnerabilities.	Leading and supporting efforts by the public and private sector to reduce threats and vulnerabilities. Threat reduction involves working with law enforcement community to investigate and prosecute cyberspace threats. Vulnerability reduction involves identifying and remediating vulnerabilities in existing software and systems.
Promote and support research and development efforts to strengthen cyberspace security.	Collaborating and coordinating with members of academia, industry, and government to optimize cybersecurity related research and development efforts to reduce vulnerabilities through the adoption of more secure technologies.
Promote awareness and outreach.	Establishing a comprehensive national awareness program to promote efforts to strengthen cybersecurity throughout government and the private sector, including the home user.
Foster training and certification.	Improving cybersecurity-related education, training, and certification opportunities.
Enhance federal, state, and local government cybersecurity.	Partnering with federal, state, and local governments in efforts to strengthen the cybersecurity of the nation's critical information infrastructure to assist in the deterrence, prevention, preemption of, and response to terrorist attacks against the United States.
Strengthen international cyberspace security.	Working in conjunction with other federal agencies, international organizations, and industry in efforts to promote strengthened cybersecurity on a global basis.
Integrate cybersecurity with national security.	Coordinating and integrating applicable national preparedness goals with its National Infrastructure Protection Plan.

Source: GAO analysis of the Homeland Security Act of 2002, the Homeland Security Presidential Directive-7, and the *National Strategy to Secure Cyberspace*.

Appendix II: Key Recommendations To Improve Cybersecurity of Critical Infrastructures

Functional Area	Recommendations That Have Not Yet Been Fully Implemented
Threat and vulnerability assessments	Perform a national cyber threat assessment.
	Facilitate sector cyber vulnerability assessments—to include identification of cross-sector interdependencies.
Strategic analysis and warning	Establish a capability for strategic analysis of computer-based threats, including developing a related methodology, acquiring staff expertise, and obtaining infrastructure data.
	Develop a comprehensive governmentwide data-collection and analysis framework and ensure that national watch and warning operations for computer-based attacks are supported by sufficient staff and resources
	Develop a comprehensive written plan for establishing analysis and warning capabilities that integrates existing planning elements and includes milestones and performance measures; approaches (or strategies) and the various resources needed to achieve the goals and objectives; a description of the relationship between the long-term goals and objectives and the annual performance goals; and a description of how program evaluations could be used to establish or revise strategic goals, along with a schedule for future program evaluations.
Infrastructure control systems protection	Develop and implement a strategy for coordinating with the private sector and other government agencies to improve control system security, including an approach for coordinating the various ongoing efforts to secure control systems.
Public/private information sharing	To ensure effective implementation of the Intelligence Reform Act, assess progress toward the milestones set in the Interim Implementation Plan; identify any barriers to achieving these milestones, such as insufficient resources and determine ways to resolve them; and recommend to the oversight committees with jurisdiction any necessary changes to the organizational structure or approach to creating the Information Sharing Environment.[26]
	Consistent with other infrastructure planning efforts such as the NIPP, define and communicate to the private sector what critical infrastructure information DHS and federal entities need to fulfill their critical infrastructure responsibilities and how federal, state, and local entities are expected to use the information submitted under the program.
	Determine whether creating mechanisms, such as providing originator control and direct submissions to federal agencies other than DHS, would increase submissions of critical infrastructure information.
	Expand efforts to use incentives to encourage more users of critical infrastructure information, such as mechanisms for state-to-state sharing.
	Proceed with and establish milestones for the development of an information-sharing plan that includes (1) a clear description of the roles and responsibilities of DHS, the ISACs, the sector coordinators, and the sector-specific agencies and (2) actions designed to address information-sharing challenges. Efforts to develop this plan should include soliciting feedback from the ISACs, sector coordinators, and sector-specific agencies to help ensure that challenges identified by the ISACs and the ISAC Council are appropriately considered in the final plan.
	Considering the roles, responsibilities, and actions established in the information-sharing plan, develop appropriate DHS policies and procedures for interacting with the Information Sharing and Analysis Centers (ISACs), sector coordinators, and sector-specific agencies and for coordination and information sharing within the IAIP Directorate (such as the National Cyber Security Division and Infrastructure Coordination Division) and other DHS components that may interact with the ISACs, including TSA.

---

[26]We made this recommendation to the Office of the Director of National Intelligence.

Functional Area	Recommendations That Have Not Yet Been Fully Implemented
Recovery planning	Establish contingency plans for cybersecurity, including recovery plans for key internet functions.
	Establish dates for revising the *National Response Plan* and finalizing the *National Infrastructure Protection Plan* (to include components related to Internet recovery).
	Draft public/private plans for Internet recovery and obtain input from key Internet infrastructure companies.
	Review the organizational structures and roles of DHS's National Communication System (NCS) and National Cyber Security Division (NCSD) in light of the convergence of voice and data communications.
	Identify the relationships and interdependencies among the various Internet recovery-related activities currently underway in NCS and NCSD.
	Establish timelines and priorities for key efforts identified by the Internet Disruption Working Group.
	Identify ways to incorporate lessons learned from actual incidents and during cyber exercises into recovery plans and procedures.
	Work with private-sector stakeholders representing the Internet infrastructure to address challenges to effective Internet recovery by (1) further defining needed government functions, (2) defining a trigger for government involvement in responding to a disruption, and (3) documenting assumptions and developing approaches to deal with key challenges that are not within the government's control.
Crosscutting topics	Engage appropriate stakeholders to prioritize key cybersecurity responsibilities so that the most important activities are addressed first.
	Prioritize a list of activities for addressing underlying challenges that are impeding execution of DHS responsibilities
	Identify performance measures and milestones for fulfilling prioritized responsibilities and activities to address underlying challenges, and track progress against these measures and milestones

Source: GAO-06-383, GAO-06-385, GAO-06-672, GAO-05-434, GAO-04-780, GAO-04-354, and GAO-01-323.

Mr. LUNGREN. Thank you very much for your testimony, from both of you.

If I knew how to work this thing, I would work it, too. Anyway, I will try and keep myself to 5 minutes.

Mr. FORESMAN. Mr. Chairman, we do have a bunch of technical experts in the room.

[Laughter.]

Mr. LUNGREN. I know that. I just don't know which button to push. I am sure it will work out.

Thank you very much for your testimony. I will give myself the first 5 minutes to ask you these questions.

Mr. Foresman, in your testimony, you acknowledge—and in the letter that I received from the secretary, dated September 12, that I received, I guess, today or last evening, in response to my letter of July 5—you acknowledge the importance of cybersecurity.

Yet, this position has remained vacant for such a long period of time. From the outside looking in, that would suggest that you don't have that really at the top of your priority list or you don't think it is important to fill it, because in the letter that I received, you indicate that, "Hey, we are still doing these things. It hasn't stopped us or slowed us down from doing it."

Why hasn't that attention been given to this?

Mr. FORESMAN. Mr. Chairman, let me address it with two points.

First, this has been the most top priority position since I came into office in January, and we have been through a number of candidates, candidates who have withdrawn from the IT industry, who found divestment of their businesses unattainable in the time-frames we needed to get them on board.

We have had individuals that have gone through the security review process and, for a variety of reasons, have not been able to continue on. But we feel confident in the candidate that we do have.

Part of this comes down to the fact that one person is absolutely critical, but not indispensable anymore than you, Mr. Chairman. If your director of constituent services leaves your office, it doesn't mean you quit doing constituent services.

We have been continuing to move forward with this, but we weren't going to simply hire someone in order to fill the position. We wanted to get a top quality candidate, get a top quality individual.

We believe that we are at that point. We felt like we were at that point several times before, but we are much further through the process this time.

Mr. LUNGREN. Mr. Powner, based on your work, it appears that DHS has not fully addressed any of its 13 key cybersecurity responsibilities. Of the 13 key responsibilities, which, from your review, should be the highest priority for DHS?

Mr. POWNER. Clearly, within those areas of responsibility, there are some core areas that should be focused on. We look at threat assessment as being one. Vulnerability assessments and reduction activities in that area would be another key one. The third one would be bolstering their analytical capability.

One of the issues in building credibility with the private sector is what does the government have that is of value to the private sector infrastructure owners. And if we had more robust analytical capability, where we were ahead of attacks, and I know the department is trying to pursue that with some of their projects, like Einstein and other things that are ongoing.

But if we offered that to the private sector, they would be more willing to participate and share information with the government.

Mr. LUNGREN. How much, if any, of the reluctance to participate—you say their lack of trust, I think is the word that you used—is the result of us not building into our legislation and our regulations protections against liability?

That is, if I am on the outside looking in, the government comes to me and says, "We would like you to share information with us with respect to the state of your cybersecurity," you may be reluctant because you may be looking at a lawsuit down the line if you are exposed as not having done everything that needs to be done, based on analysis done by the department.

Do you have any sense of that?

Mr. POWNER. Well, we clearly hear that from some of the infrastructure owners that that is one reason why they do not provide any information.

The second reason is, you know, they provide information, but what do they get back in return? If you don't get something in return, you are less willing to provide that.

Although I will say, in all fairness to the department, they recently issued a rule which is associated with how critical infrastructure information is shared and there is greater clarity in terms of how that information is handled and protected on the government side.

So that was clearly a step in the right direction that recently occurred.

Mr. LUNGREN. Mr. Foresman, there is criticism, obviously, that you have not fully addressed any of the 13 key cybersecurity responsibilities.

What would you say in response to that, number one? And, number two, how do you prioritize among those 13 in terms of what you need to do at the department?

Mr. FORESMAN. Mr. Chairman, what I would say is we very much acknowledge the great work that the Government Accountability Office continues to do on a wide range of fronts and the recommendations that Mr. Powner has brought forward are ones that will help us chart the road ahead.

But to the second piece of it, in terms of prioritization, this is not simply unilateral action on the part of the Department of Homeland Security.

One of the reasons why we have a wide range of constituencies involved in this process, public sector and private sector, sector coordinating council, just being one of many examples, as we are working through the national infrastructure protection plan in the IT sector, is so that we can bring the private sector stakeholders to the table with government and in an environment of collaboration to make a mutual determination about where the priorities are, because if we in the department were to have a priority that was different than, say, the Office of Management and Budget at the federal level or the state of New York at the state level or

Microsoft at the corporate level, we are not going to be headed in the same direction.

So this is not the easiest environment in the world, because it is not a regulated environment. It shouldn't be a regulated environment. And we have got to create a mutually shared vision and gain a wide range of consensus.

And, clearly, one of the things that we know is that there are market factors that can be brought into play that will incentivize. You mentioned liability, just being one of many.

Mr. LUNGREN. My time, I believe, has expired. When we come back, I want to ask you about the three top priorities specifically.

The gentlelady?

Ms. SANCHEZ. Thank you, gentlemen, for being before us.

You know, it is not just a lack of this assistant secretary that you have been unable to fill for the last year. I mean, the GAO noted, in its last report, in 2005, that there were various people who had left the department and that there really is no leadership going on.

And my question is how can you say that because you haven't filled that position, you—I mean, there seems to be no leadership in this area.

In fact, I think your report noted that some of the industry groups you had spoken to said that the lack of these positions being filled really noted a lack of leadership from that department.

Is that not true?

Mr. FORESMAN. Yes, that is true. What we heard from certain infrastructure owners was the lack of leadership was sending a message that it was not an administration priority.

Ms. SANCHEZ. So is it an administration priority?

Mr. FORESMAN. Ms. Sanchez, it is, in fact, an administration priority. When Secretary Chertoff went through the second stage review and we created this position, we did it in response to a desire on the part of the industry and a desire on the part of Congress, as well as the federal executive branch, to have greater collaboration and coordination.

And I acknowledge and I am the first one to acknowledge that this has been a tough process to get this position filled.

And, Congresswoman, I want to say it is not for wont of trying. We have been working exceptionally hard and, as you know, the department—it is hard to recruit, frankly, because there is great criticism of the department on many fronts.

And many of the folks who have the IT background are making very substantial salaries in the private sector and you have to make a sacrifice to come into government and it has been difficult to find individuals willing to make the sacrifice.

Ms. SANCHEZ. I think a lot of us make a sacrifice to come into the government.

Mr. DICKS. Would you yield just for one question?

On that very point, do you have an acting assistant secretary? We have acting secretaries all over the government. Is there an acting assistant secretary?

Mr. FORESMAN. Congressman, there is. And we had Bob Stephan, who was our assistant secretary for infrastructure protection, was dual hatted, carrying the responsibilities of doing infrastructure protection, also overseeing the efforts of our cybersecurity and our national communications systems activities.

Recently, we interjected the deputy undersecretary for preparedness, Rob Zitz, who works for me, to provide for the day-to-day management and oversight, in collaboration with the national cybersecurity division and the national communications system, simply because of the fact that we are going through trying to get the national infrastructure protection plan done, get all the sector coordination plans done.

And Bob was doing yeoman's work with both hats on, but we have added an additional person in there to help make sure that the folks in both of these shops have the tools, the resources and the guidance necessary to be successful.

Mr. DICKS. Thank you.

Ms. SANCHEZ. Certainly, Mr. Dicks.

So you are telling me that he was—did you officially do that? Because we never got word that you did this. You titled him with the acting secretary position?

Mr. FORESMAN. We did not. What I am saying to you is—

Ms. SANCHEZ. You just said you were going to give it all over to him to do.

Mr. FORESMAN. No, ma'am. What we have said is that Mr. Zitz has the responsibility for ensuring day-to-day oversight and coordination efforts between the national cybersecurity division, as well as the national communications system.

Ms. SANCHEZ. Okay, I think the question that Mr. Dicks had was did you have an acting assistant secretary for cybersecurity and telecommunications.

Mr. FORESMAN. We did and that is Mr. Steffen.

Ms. SANCHEZ. So he is doing both secretary positions.

Mr. FORESMAN. He is doing both secretary positions. And, Congresswoman, he is on paper today doing the cybersecurity and the communications system in the context that Bob was working phenomenal hours, trying to do both jobs, and we added a second person in to provide day-to-day direction and oversight.

Ms. SANCHEZ. Well, this is such an important job. I mean, I can't imagine that someone is going to have a real full-time job and then take this job on.

And you can really sit there with a straight face and tell me that he was doing both jobs.

Mr. FORESMAN. Congresswoman, my—

Ms. SANCHEZ. That is like saying I am a congresswoman and Mr. Lungren's district doesn't have a congressperson, therefore, I am going to be the acting one. I mean, it is two jobs you just can't do together.

Mr. FORESMAN. Well, Congresswoman, let me just offer this. In the context of providing advice and counsel to the men and women of both of these shops, providing strategic direction and leadership, we have plenty of folks who are available and are doing that on a day-to-day basis.

Ms. SANCHEZ. Did you have a comment?

Mr. LUNGREN. Well, if the gentlelady would yield for a second.

Mr. Foresman, could you tell us when you do anticipate filling this position?

Mr. FORESMAN. Congressman, as you know, the individual who will fill this position will have access to some of the most highly classified data that is available. They are going through the security clearance process.

The way I would best characterize it is in terms of where one would normally expect them to be in the security clearance review process. They are way beyond that point, which shows that we are making getting the security clearance done a highest priority.

Mr. LUNGREN. So is the answer that the only thing holding this up is the finalization of the security clearance?

Mr. FORESMAN. That is correct.

Ms. SANCHEZ. I want to talk about compensation for a minute, because we had the whole issue of Andy Purdy and being paid from different pots.

Do you think that you have adequate protections in place to deal with potential conflicts of interest that arise when the IPA contractors oversee business arrangements between the government and their home employer?

Mr. FORESMAN. Congresswoman, we do, but beyond that step, as you know, the department used a large number of IPAs in the early days to get the department up and running.

We made a very deliberate decision and in consultation with the secretary and the deputy secretary, when I came on board, we are moving as many of the current IPA positions to full-time federal employee positions, recognizing that we are transitioning from what one would reasonably say is the startup point of the department, where IPAs were a necessity, to the point of where we need to convert these to full-time federal employees.

Ms. SANCHEZ. So how many IPAs would you estimate are still around? And I am assuming what you are telling me is that you are moving them from however many you might have right now to a net of zero.

You don't really want IPAs hanging around in the department?

Mr. FORESMAN. No, Congresswoman, I wouldn't say that we are going to do it at a 100 percent. There is going to be a necessity for IPAs particularly in selected expertise areas, high science areas.

But for the vast majority of positions that were IPA before, we are taking a very hard look at this and, frankly, we want to make sure that we had these as full-time federal employees, not subject to the provisions of some of the limitations that, frankly, are placed on IPAs, because they don't fit into that full-time federal employee status.

Ms. SANCHEZ. Thank you, Mr. Chairman.

Mr. LUNGREN. The time of the gentlelady has expired.

The gentleman from the state of Washington is recognized for 5 minutes.

Mr. DICKS. Well, thank you.

You have got this person that you signed a 2-year contract with, Andy Purdy, is that correct?

Mr. FORESMAN. That is correct.

Mr. DICKS. And 2 years to serve as acting director of the national cybersecurity division.

Mr. FORESMAN. That is correct.

Mr. DICKS. In a time when enduring leadership over the federal government's effort in this arena is vital, why would the department sign a two-year contract that expressly provides for an interim director?

Mr. FORESMAN. Congressman, I will have to offer that that occurred before my arrival, but what I will say is that upon my arrival, upon my assumption of the duties and the responsibilities, we have looked at our IPA activities and I want to convert these over to FTE, full-time federal employee positions, and we are in the process of doing that.

Mr. DICKS. Now, we know that the preparedness directorate also uses IPAs, as was mentioned. A recent news article revealed that acting NCSD director Andy Purdy receives a $277,000 salary, mostly paid by the department, all while overseeing a multi-million dollar budget for this home institution of Carnegie Mellon.

Does the preparedness directorate have adequate protections in place to deal with potential conflicts of interest?

Mr. FORESMAN. Congressman, as you know, this issue did come up in the public, in the press over the course of the last several months, and we went and did an exhaustive review of it.

When Andy came on board, he was subjected to the same ethics requirements that the rest of the federal employees are subjected to. We have a series of checks and balances.

We have separate business functions from those who oversee program activities. And we do feel like it was adequate.

Mr. DICKS. The Cybersecurity Alliance have called for increased funding of cybersecurity efforts within the department. Yet, the administration lowered the budget by several hundred thousand dollars this year and the Senate Homeland Appropriations Committee recommended a decrease of almost $10 million for the budget request for 2007.

Why is cybersecurity having such a hard time obtaining proper funding from the administration and from the majority party in the Senate?

Mr. FORESMAN. Congressman, I think I would articulate it like this. We shouldn't measure our success or failure with cybersecurity efforts in dollars spent, but rather in the ability to leverage the resources.

As a for instance, one of the things that the GAO report mentions in terms of the analytical ability—Mr. Chairman, this goes to one of your three top priorities—is enhancing our analytical ability.

Part of that hinges on leveraging better the intelligence community. And I will tell you, Congressman, that as we look across the spectrum of things that we are doing on our cybersecurity efforts, we are trying to break down the stovepipes inside the department so that we don't have, if you will, two activities doing the same function.

The Secret Service does elements of cyber training. Their cybersecurity division is involved in cyber training. And we are looking to achieve efficiencies where we can merge activities and get more bang for the buck.

So I would not articulate that dollars spent is a clear indicator of whether we are being successful or not with our cybersecurity efforts.

Mr. DICKS. Well, Mr. Powner, you are the GAO fellow, right?

Mr. POWNER. Correct.

Mr. DICKS. I missed your presentation, but you guys have done studies over the last several years and it is still your impression that we are not making very much progress in terms of getting this area moving forward.

Mr. POWNER. Well, if you look comprehensively at the whole plan for tackling the cyber critical infrastructure protection arena, we can go back to 1996, with Presidential Directive 63. We haven't made much progress.

We put a lot of plans—

Ms. SANCHEZ. May I ask a question related to that?

Mr. DICKS. Let him finish his answer. Then I will yield to you.

Mr. POWNER. I mean, we put resources and there are always plans in place, but we need to get off of putting plans in place and actually get down to implementation.

We are going to get sector-specific plans, hopefully, at the end of the year, that are tied to the national infrastructure protection plan. Hopefully, those plans move us beyond another plan, but more into vulnerability assessments, efforts to protect our infrastructure, efforts to reduce the vulnerabilities that are out there, and, also, to put in place recovery plans.

We don't have those things, if you look at—individual companies do, yes, but if you look at sector by sector and what is called for in law and policy, we do not have those.

Mr. DICKS. I yield.

Ms. SANCHEZ. Do you think they have a vision? I mean, with nobody at the top really under this and with so many people having come in and been cyber czar, as I call them, I think the fifth person now.

I mean, do the people that work in this area and does the department really have a vision about what they are supposed to be doing or do you find them struggling?

Mr. POWNER. Clearly, they are struggling, in aspects. But in terms of a vision, there is a national infrastructure protection plan that has a lot of the right pieces in place. It calls for the right things, to engage the right parties.

Now, what we need to do is to engage those parties and move forward on the implementation phase. So I would say the national infrastructure protection plan, a lot of the aspects of that plan are pretty good, but now the challenge becomes in implementing it and it is tough to implement it when you have this history of not necessarily having the strongest relationship with various sectors in the private sector who own the majority of the infrastructure.

It is a huge challenge.

Ms. SANCHEZ. Thank you, Mr. Dicks.

Mr. DICKS. Let me ask you these. We spent a lot of money in the Department of Defense looking at cybersecurity from a Defense Department perspective. I serve on Defense Appropriations. Has DHS benefited at all from the work that was done at the DOD?

Mr. POWNER. A couple comments. I think, clearly, we could leverage other aspects of the federal government where we have made progress. DOD, if you look at their defense cybersecurity lab, if you look at their joint task force, they have got many areas that look at cyber initiatives.

And I think the department has acknowledged that trying to link up and leverage those aspects within the Department of Defense and build a partnership in those areas are needed.

Mr. DICKS. Mr. Chairman, just one quick, last, brief question.

Mr. LUNGREN. Sure, go right ahead.

Mr. DICKS. Thank you.

Mr. Foresman, did the DHS ethics officer approve the Purdy arrangement?

Mr. FORESMAN. Congressman, I believe he did, but let me confirm that and provide you a written response.

Mr. DICKS. Get us a response. And if there was a letter written at the time, we would like to have that, if that would be all right with the chairman.

Mr. LUNGREN. That would be fine.

Mr. DICKS. I think we need to be able to see a copy of what was sent at the time.

Does the GAO know anything about that?

Mr. POWNER. No, sir.

Mr. DICKS. Thank you. Thank you, Mr. Chairman.

Mr. LUNGREN. The gentleman's time has expired.

The gentleman from Indiana is recognized for 5 minutes.

Mr. SOUDER. I appreciate your testimony and the unbelievable complexity of the challenge.

I had kind of a side question, but I wonder how it is extending the front that you have to defend.

I know in the GAO testimony, you have about how to protect government computers and there is a reference also to the university names that were stolen and others.

But in the Veterans a Administration, where we, in effect, had most of our veterans a, a high percentage of our veterans a names appeared to have been stolen in a random burglary, because it went home and the computer went home, and, at one point, it looked like we might have even compromised home addresses and our active servicemen, meaning that they would be vulnerable.

How does the whole experience of contracting out, not only in the government arena, but in the private arena—are you looking at how to build—I understand the veterans a department is trying to work additional firewalls in.

How are we going to handle this without, in effect, pulling everything back inside a few walls? This is like making our entire system vulnerable at its weakest link, which is at home. It is vulnerable to random robberies, penetrations of some kid hacker on his dad's computer.

Mr. FORESMAN. Congressman, let me start and maybe Mr. Powner may have additional comments. This actually very much underscores the complexity of probably among our greatest vulnerabilities is not on our networks, as I think some of your next panels of witnesses will talk about, but in the context of the computer sitting on the desk at home or in the small business office somewhere.

And, you know, this becomes the same challenge that we have when we talk about how do we prepare America for emergencies and disasters of any kind and part of this comes back to citizen education.

You know, October is national cybersecurity awareness month and just as much as we want the average citizen to know that they need to check their smoke detector batteries in October, we also want our citizens to know that you can at buy the computer, you can't load the software on it, and you can't say, "Okay, I am good forever on until I get the next computer."

And it requires maintenance, it requires work, and this is one of the areas where I think strong collaboration between the public sector and the private sector, constant messaging is going to be absolutely critical.

Mr. POWNER. Just to second that, when you look at security as a whole, it is only as good as your weakest link.

We do a lot of work not only looking at cyber critical infrastructure, but looking at individual agencies and departments. We have a lab internally that we attempt to break into systems and networks in federal departments and agencies and we are almost always successful.

But there are simple things, like when you are not successful, we will call the Department of Homeland Security and say, "We are working for Mr. Foresman and he forgot his password and can you give it to us." And you know what? We usually get it.

So it is those type of things, too, and it makes it very difficult, because you have got this huge technological component that you have to secure, but it is also relying on the individuals and the people, too.

And educating everyone and having that whole picture in place is very difficult with many of these departments.

Mr. SOUDER. Well, thank you for scaring me even more. Mr. Chairman, I want to point out, I have blue and gold on.

Mr. LUNGREN. That is very good. I am just painting my office blue and gold, after the victory against Penn State, I guess it was. Now it is Michigan, the next one coming up.

The gentlelady from the great state of Texas is recognized for 5 minutes.

Ms. JACKSON-LEE. Well, you know, I am stuck in orange and we are struggling, but we are going to make it.

Mr. LUNGREN. I wasn't going to say a thing.

Ms. JACKSON-LEE. But thank you very much, Mr. Chairman, to the ranking member.

I am going to use a part of my time to try to articulate some of the piquing frustration. As I do that, Mr. Foresman, I do want to acknowledge that you are a superb professional. We thank you for your service.

We thank Mr. Powner, as well, and the GAO is certainly one of our frequent witnesses throughout the Congress.

But I notice that this room is particularly tranquil and very well appointed and would give us a sense of calm. Here is my frustration.

We are not living in a calm arena. Day to day, we are noting the use of technology, levels of sophistication by Al Qaida, certainly the new sophisticated creative uses of mere liquids that would create havoc in the nations and the world skies, and, of course, as my colleague mentioned, the ludicrous incident or accident of a missing laptop and thousands upon thousands of veterans a personal information.

I just had a hearing yesterday on the National Security Agency and, of course, the issues dealing with warrantless searches, which speaks to corporations who are now either engaged or not engaged in providing data, issues of data mining.

These are major issues and I guess as I look at this structure that you have, I am a little—we call it unready, a great deal of discomfort.

Mr. Purdy may be a very fine professional himself, but I am listening to Mr. Powner, who said he is completely blank on this arrangement.

My concern would be attention span and the ability to run a multi-conglomerate, whatever responsibility Mr. Purdy has, whether or not he has put it in trust, I am not sure, and this very important responsibility.

I do hear you saying that there is a process going and someone is being embedded as we speak.

But I think the message I want you to take back to Secretary Chertoff, and we had great hopes and dreams for homeland security, we still do, we wouldn't be here, committed, as you heard, that there has to be a certain energy, a certain sense of urgency, a certain sense of panic, that we wouldn't have to see one area after another be vacant, be with acting or interim.

And we are all sort of facing those uphill obstacles. You are not the personnel director, of course, but I think it is important to note that the idea of staffing is crucial.

So maybe you can give me a sense of who is working under Mr. Purdy. What kind of shop do we have there? Vision has never been—it is good planning, but it has never been answers to terrorism, because we can visioning for a long time and subject the American people to a major, if you will, terrorist attack.

We are all sort of sitting on edge because we know that just by the nature of this heinous business now that is going on the world, that we are certainly as vulnerable as the next. We are trying to secure this nation, but we have a lot of gaping holes.

So tell me what staffing you have and what are you practically doing as it relates to cybersecurity, because you have got an interim person?

And, Mr. Powner, in my closing moment, would you then take it to the next level of what are the Achilles heels as we are presently structured? The interim person, maybe some of your questions not being answered, in a world of cybersecurity.

And I yield to you, Mr. Foresman.

Mr. FORESMAN. Congresswoman, thank you for the question. And let me also, to the context of what Congressman Dicks asked about, I did get a note from staff and the ethics officer did review the arrangement before Mr. Purdy came on board. So it did go through the ethics review process, but we will provide any additional clarity that you wish.

I would generally break four primary functions in the national cybersecurity division and some of the most talented men and women and very dedicated men and women, and I would invite all of you all to come out to the U.S. CERT center out in Northern Virginia and see what they do every day to monitor what is going on across the Internet, to identify and look for vulnerabilities.

Ms. JACKSON-LEE. Do you know the numbers of your staff, how many are out there?

Mr. FORESMAN. I can get you an approximate. Congresswoman, I don't know off—

Ms. JACKSON-LEE. But is every spot filled?

Mr. FORESMAN. I believe that they are close, because we are making sure vacancies—

Ms. JACKSON-LEE. You are making headway.

Mr. FORESMAN. Minimizing vacancies. But there are four primary buckets. One is kind of the detection and monitoring. That is the U.S. CERT folks. That is the operational piece, knowing what is going on, having a place that the federal interagency and the private sector can reach into 24/7 to be able to do it.

The second category is those efforts that are targeted towards raising education and awareness across the university sector and that type of activity.

The third area is what is traditionally the planning, getting the private sector and the public sector folks in the room together and making sure that we know how we are going to respond to a threat, we know how we are going to respond to an actual event, we know how we are going to implement recovery.

And those are the folks who had the hard time of translating the idea for greater cooperation.

Ms. JACKSON-LEE. And your team is engaged in information sharing. You are part of the component that deals with the information sharing component. I assume that you look at information.

Are you the gatherers or are you providing information out?

Mr. FORESMAN. Well, it is both. It is really both being—

Ms. JACKSON-LEE. You are functioning in two ways. You feel confident that you are functioning now with your staff.

Mr. FORESMAN. We are functioning, but, Congresswoman, I am not going to mislead you or this committee. We got our high track activity, which is a collaborative activity that is responsible for getting intelligence information out to the private sector and getting it back in and feeding it into the intelligence community.

We have got the work of the U.S. CERT. We have got our national operations center, the national coordination center for telecommunications. They are closer and better tied than they were a year ago. They are closer and much better tied than they were 4 years ago or 3 years ago, when the department was stood up.

But we still have more work to do and we need to make sure it is a seamless operation. One of the things I said earlier in my testimony was we are going to put the telecommunications coordinating group that is there 24/7 right next to the information technology, the cybersecurity group that is there 24/7, because the telecommunications infrastructure and our information technology infrastructure are inextricably related and we want to make sure that those folks are sitting next to each other when things go on so that they can share that information back and forth.

Ms. JACKSON-LEE. Mr. Chairman, if you will indulge me, so that Mr. Powner could respond, please.

Thank you. Thank you, Mr. Foresman.

Mr. POWNER. Congresswoman, clearly, there are—getting at the human capital issue within the department there, clearly, there are many capable men and women within the national cybersecurity division. Many of them are sitting in this room today. We just need more of them.

In terms of leadership, though, there is a leadership void. We need a permanent leader not only for the department internally, but because of the interaction with the private sector, the state and local governments.

So we clearly need that. This isn't the only department that has struggled with getting capable folks on board. I do work in many areas across the federal government. IRS is an example.

They had a huge human capital issue there, not being able to deliver. I can say today, looking at them over a number of years, they have one of the better IT organizations when it comes to their modernization efforts.

They still have hiccups, but how did they do that? They got critical position pay, where they paid folks above the SES salary cap. So there are things you could do and you could pursue.

It is not perfect, because it is still difficult to compete with the private sector salaries, but there are things you could do and you could pursue and there are some good examples out there in other federal departments that we could move forward on.

Ms. JACKSON-LEE. Thank you.

To you, Mr. Chairman, I would just say those of us who live beyond the beltway, I would really like to give an SOS e-mail to our friends here in Washington to start going out and recruiting across the country, whether it is Texas or California or Washington state.

We have got to be able to find good people and good people are out there and there must be some recruiting blindness, but we need to start reaching out to our own constituents, because they are out there and they know this business.

And I yield back. Thank you.

Mr. LUNGREN. I thank the gentlelady. We will do a second round with this panel before we go to the second panel.

Mr. Foresman, you were going to tell me what the three top priorities are regarding cybersecurity responsibilities? You gave us one, which is enhancing analytical abilities.

What would the other two be?

Mr. FORESMAN. Congressman, clearly, it is the ability to effect the coordination between the agencies of the federal government with our state and local partners and between government and the private sector, just the basic operational coordination.

And then the second one is information sharing. As Mr. Powner pointed out, there has got to be a tangible benefit to the private sector and this is not just limited to the information technology sector. This is across all of our critical, whether we are talking about ports in transportation systems or our IT systems.

What is the value added for the private sector to share information with government and, conversely, government has got to—it has got to be a two-way street.

Mr. LUNGREN. I mean, part of this hearing is, obviously, beating up on you, because the department hasn't done as much as it needs to do in this area. But, look, I am going to confess, the Congress hasn't either.

If there is one area that we probably lag behind in terms of the array of vulnerabilities we have, in my judgment, more than anything else, it is probably cybersecurity.

But we will keep sending these letters to you and we will still keep prodding you to do these things.

Mr. DICKS. Mr. Chairman, didn't we have national commission on cybersecurity? That, I thought, did an outstanding effort. I mean, this issue has been out there.

Mr. LUNGREN. I am not saying the issue hasn't been out there. What I am suggesting is, I mean, as I look at the Congress, I am not sure that we have done what we need to do.

Mr. DICKS. In terms of oversight?

Mr. LUNGREN. In terms of oversight, in terms of prodding the department. I just want to let you know we are going to be doing a much stronger job on that. We are going to be inviting you to come up here more often.

We are going to be sending letters out. We are going to make inquiries. We need to get moving on this.

This is not as visible as a physical piece of critical infrastructure, yet it is as important, if not more important, because it is embedded in and underlies so much of what we do.

And in that regard, I would ask you about the SCADA systems, the control systems that we have. They are so critical, as they provide a link between the cyber world and the physical world. These need to be a top priority.

Does the department have a specific plan to work with various critical infrastructure sectors to protect their control systems, to actually get it done? As Mr. Powner said, we have done a lot of studies, a lot of planning.

Are we actually doing it?

Mr. FORESMAN. Congressman, three quick points on that. First, we are looking, as we are doing all of the sector plans, whether it is the chemical sector or the dam sector, all of these other ones that have SCADA systems that we are concerned about.

We have got a cyber component that is built in as they go about doing their sector coordination. The sector coordinating councils develop their sector-specific plans and then part of this is having them say what is the best practice, what is the acceptable standard that we are promoting and pushing within a particular sector and having that implemented.

The second piece is training and education and I think you and this committee undoubtedly understand the SCADA issues as well as any group out there and there is a growing need to educate.

As a matter of fact, here at the end of the month, there is a session that we are going to be teaching out in Las Vegas in conjunction with a conference, where we are going to focus exclusively on the SCADA issues and protection and prevention measures associated with it.

And then the third part of it is there is a business issue here. You know, if you think about SCADA systems, the control systems back pre–a92–a93, when we saw the major proliferation of information technology, the older systems tend not to be as reliant on the Internet as those that are built into the current systems.

And a lot of this is we have to make the business case to corporate America that protection of their SCADA systems goes back to what you talked about earlier, the liability issue. What is the acceptable national standard by which someone will be judged as it relates to the protection of SCADA systems?

And, frankly, I think that market-driven incentives rather than overt, heavy-handed regulation is going to get us there, but there is a liability issue for corporate America and we need to make sure that we articulate that.

Mr. LUNGREN. And one of the things we have to do, from our standpoint, working with your department, is to ensure that we know that the landscape is out there. How can we get the information from the various sectors dealing with their own cybersecurity?

How are we going to develop the trust such that they will give us that information, so that we can utilize it, so that we can make a better judgment here in the Congress as to what makes sense from a legislative standpoint as opposed to what makes sense from a regulatory standpoint as opposed to what makes sense from an incentive standpoint as opposed to what makes sense from the risk management experts, which is the insurance industry?

If we don't have that information, we may be heavy-handed on the regulatory side or the statutory side only because we don't have that information.

So we have to build a relationship of trust with the private sector so that they will feel free to share that information with us, feel free to share it with you.

That is not an easy thing to do, even with the question of liability. But beyond that, do they trust us to have the competence to be able to deal with the information they give us?

So I am looking at this not to point fingers at people. I am looking at this to solve a problem. And when we are given the responsibility in this committee and this subcommittee of dealing with critical infrastructure, it seems to me, if we don't look at cybersecurity as a part of that, we are not doing our job.

And we are like a non-modern governmental entity trying to deal with a modern world. It just isn't going to work.

So we will be pressing and working hard and we will do this on a bipartisan basis, because I know the concern is shared by both Democrats and Republicans.

All right, if I can get this working again, I will start it off for another 5 minutes for my ranking member, the gentlelady from California.

Ms. SANCHEZ. Thank you, Mr. Chairman. I just want to say that one of the reasons that we may have not been paying as much attention lately to cybersecurity is, as you will recall, when we first started the Homeland Security Committee, we had an actual subcommittee that dealt with cybersecurity.

And then the reorg that happened in the last 2 years, this was put under the jurisdiction of this subcommittee, which, as you know, has an extensive portfolio and trying to get through TSA and ports and everything else.

I guess this may be the second hearing that we have had on cybersecurity in the 2 years.

So it is important to get done. I just don't know how we also will find the time. It is always a difficult thing to do.

And there are some good things that have come out of the directorate. As you know, when we have been in the markup sessions, I have tried to put more money into some of the programs that I think have been done well.

So for me, it is more of understanding that we have had this revolving door at the top and the frustration of not being able to fill it and the idea of the people, the rest of the people in the agency having less direction than they probably need to get things done.

So that is why we are so, I think, concerned to see this issue of filling the slots with competent people who want to stay around, which we see in a lot of the different areas of homeland security. It is a major problem. And the morale issues and the pay issues and everything that go with it.

And just, you know, developing something new, it takes a special kind of person. A lot of people can follow, but it is hard to lead. So we really need to fill those leadership positions.

The GAO said that progress to date on initiatives to improve the nation's ability to recover from Internet disruption, that the progress had been limited and that other initiatives lacked timeframes for completion, and, also, that the relationships between these initiatives are not evident.

Can you tell me what efforts must be made by the department to achieve the kinds of relationships that need to exist for these initiatives to work? Again, the ones that deal with working groups to facilitate coordination and exercises in which government and the private industry practice respond to cyber events.

Mr. FORESMAN. Congresswoman, I think there are three really big issues here. One is clear deliverable timelines and I will tell you, this is an issue—you noted correctly that the department continues to go through growing pains, but we have gotten through that first visceral reaction of getting the department up and running.

And we do need to take a collective deep breath and look at all of the things that we are doing and make sure and make sure what we are doing is still what we need to be doing this time next week, but that we are putting specific deliverable timelines on these.

And I think part of this, and I talked to Mr. Powner ahead of time, when we get the new assistant secretary on board, I would like to sit down with the GAO and amalgamate all of the recommendations across the cyber front and develop a matrix.

I am not going to say we are going to do them all, but there is a lot of great work that has gone in there. There is a lot of great work that is coming out of the sector coordinating councils.

One of the advantages is we are working with the business sector. They don't do well if we don't have clear, definitive end products that we are looking for and timelines. So they are helping to push us. That is the first thing.

The second piece of it really comes down to the issue of trust that we have talked about. And I want to be clear, when we talk about trust, these types of public-private sector relationships, even going back to PDD–63 in the 1990s timeframe, and 67, this is new. Government has always been a regulator and private sector has always been a regulatee.

So we are talking about new relationships here. The PCII rule, the protecting critical infrastructure information, the tool that this Congress gave to the department, a very important tool, we have taken, we have implemented just here in the last several months, and it provides an additional layer of competence to the private sector that key information that they provide to us is not going to end up out in the public domain, particularly where we are talking about proprietary information, because you know one bad piece of information affects stock prices and we understand that.

So I am anxious to see how the PCII rule, married together with our ongoing relationships, provides tangible benefits as we go forward.

And then the third piece of it is I think it is going to come back to as we define and continue to work with Congress on this issue, we have got a national strategy on securing cyberspace. That is the high level document.

As Mr. Powner said, we have got the national infrastructure protection plan, the next level down. We have got the sector coordination plans that are being put—the sector-specific plans that are being put together.

But we have got to get down into the implementation level and that is what normally would come next in the cycle. That is what is normally going to come next in the cycle, but I will tell you I don't want to be up here 6 months from now telling you all we haven't made progress.

I would like to be able to appear before this subcommittee and say here are the 15 or 20 things—or, actually, I would like to have the assistant secretary appear before you all and say here are the 15 or 20 things that have gotten done in the last 6 months and, by the way, here are the 15 or 20 things that the private sector agrees with us that we are going to do in the next 6 months.

Ms. SANCHEZ. Mr. Powner, do you have anything you might want to enlighten us on that?

Mr. POWNER. Just one comment about the whole trust issue. There is a lot of discussion about building trust and I think naming the secretary position, that will be great going forward.

But we don't build trust through individuals or because we are competent or a good person in this position. You are going to build trust with the private sector because the government is going to have something that is of value to them.

And right now we need to grow the capability in the government to offer something that is of value. That is ultimately how you are going to build trust.

I have spent some time in the telecommunications sector and, I will tell you, when I was there, we didn't share a lot with the government, because the ultimate question was what benefit is that to our company.

If we are interested in stock prices, when we have someone we wanted prosecuted because they were in our central office, that is when we wanted the government assistance, because they could help us.

He key question is building trust. I think we go back to that analytical capability and some of the key items that are called for, called for in policy and in law. If we start tackling some of those key priorities, we can build trust.

It is difficult, but I think there are some things that are in place that we can march forward with.

Ms. SANCHEZ. Thank you.

Mr. LUNGREN. Thank you.

The gentleman from Indiana is recognized for 5 minutes.

Mr. SOUDER. First, I wanted to say something about the Cybersecurity Subcommittee here. That is, first, I want to thank the speaker for giving us any flexibility at all to do cybersecurity.

The Energy and Commerce Committee has been trying to muscle this committee and we need to push back. In every session of Congress, we need to work to make sure jurisdiction for homeland security stays under this committee.

It is a wonder that we have had any jurisdiction, given how hard they went after our committee on that.

Mr. LUNGREN. If the gentleman would yield on that.

One of the points I have been trying to make is if cybersecurity is not part and parcel of critical infrastructure, I don't know what is. And I didn't come back here to have fights with other committees, but we need to do our job and we cannot do our job in terms of critical infrastructure protection if we do not involve ourselves in an major way in terms of cybersecurity.

Mr. SOUDER. There are members of Congress in both political parties that would love to see the death of this committee and we need to fight.

Ms. SANCHEZ. Will the gentleman yield for one second?

When I was talking about the history of this, what I meant is it is so critical. I mean, it warranted its own subcommittee before. It is very important.

Mr. SOUDER. Because my concern was that we weren't going to have any jurisdiction whatsoever, because that was why we initially eliminated the cybersecurity, because we had that.

Energy and Commerce tried to make a move to exclude us from having any jurisdiction and the chairman and the committee and the subcommittee chairman here has put some cybersecurity in, because we are all in agreement here what we need to do is make sure that this committee—because if you don't have cybersecurity, everything else falls apart.

As the chairman just said, we are acting like we are in the dark ages here. This is where they are talking the stories that you have in here on the worms and what can happen at nuclear power plants, what happens if our electrical grid shuts down, the internal security of the United States.

There are lots of things that people just assume are protected. I felt the most scaring, eye-opening hearing—it wasn't a hearing— a briefing that I had was with the cybersecurity subcommittee under this, when we first created homeland security, and we had the guy who had originally been the attacker of our systems and now the defender of our Defense Department systems.

I just can't see anything other than that repeated, firewalls with incredible strength to feel off different parts, we are never going to be able to protect everything, is, in my book, the number one thing that has to be done.

How that can be done on the Internet, surely, we have to have the ability to cut this off, much like if the bird flu hits, how you are going to have to do segmentation of society like we did in 1916 with the flu epidemic.

You have to be able to isolate this stuff more rapidly than we are doing.

But I had a couple other particular questions. I would be interested if you agree that that is the biggest challenge, is how to wall it off when we get hit.

But one is clearly staffing and you are competing in an industry that pays incredible amounts of money, trying to keep people long term, divest stocks that they have, it is a huge challenge.

Have you been looking at innovative payroll type things, that if somebody stays a period longer, they get a bonus? In other words, tier the pay somewhat on how long they are there.

Should we be looking at personnel things that change? Because this is not a typical department. And I don't see, in the future, that there is going to be less demand for people with high skill cybersecurity and we don't want to have basically the people who couldn't quite cut it out in the rating field trying to defend us from the people who want to attack us, because there is incredible amounts of money to be made by attacking a system.

And a second part of this is that as I was alluding to earlier and you correctly said, the weakest part of the system is our vulnerability.

As we look at contracting out, as companies diversify and you have all these different modes of operation, are we looking at requiring different security systems for the level of the vulnerability of the site that you are at and putting in requirements and penalties if you fail to do that?

In other words, yes, we need cooperation. I am a free market businessperson who wants to see cooperation. But there are certain things that the society assumes are happening.

And the question is how do we put in certain safeguards, because now it isn't just your business, you can endanger everybody in the United States because you got sloppy.

What are we doing in putting in standards that if you are going to have access that can get you into one of these networks, particularly if we are a little uncertain of our wall, to do that?

Mr. FORESMAN. Congressman, let me maybe give three points, and I don't know whether Mr. Powner might want to add something, as well.

But I would also suggest that your next panel, I think, could address that same question and give some good clarity to it.

The first part, in terms of filling this position, I have looked at every innovative human resource opportunity that we can and there is nobody in the city of Washington who wants this position filled more than the undersecretary for preparedness at the Department of Homeland Security, for a whole bunch of reasons.

But to one of the things that Congresswoman Sanchez said, we made it very clear that whoever was going to sign up with this was going to sign up for the long term, because we didn't need a revolving door and that would have been the worst thing for industry.

So we put some strong parameters on it. Please come serve the nation and, oh, by the way, you have got to be here for the long haul, and that did scare some people off, in addition to the things you have mentioned.

But we are restricted by law in certain categories, but we have tried to be innovative.

To the second point, I think I would very much offer to you that industry has shown tremendous progress at developing, if you will, acceptable standards and practices, but they are not universally adopted across all industries.

So part of this is going to be the ongoing dialogue and discussion with the private sector about how do we get universal compliance. Is it going to be through market-driven incentives, through insurance? Is it going to be through regulation?

We don't know the answer to that, but I will offer to you that I have met very few folks in the technology community that don't understand the vulnerabilities. But as one person said at a session this morning, you have got to compare the bottom line and the needs of the moment.

And these are tough decisions and I think we may need to provide some structural policy incentives to make it all happen, but ultimately, the same that we develop the Internet through innovation, we probably need to develop increased security through innovation.

Mr. LUNGREN. The time of the gentleman has expired.

The gentleman from Washington is recognized for 5 minutes.

Mr. DICKS. Thank you, Mr. Chairman.

I want to go back to this question about Andy Purdy. As we understand, as I said, he earns $245,000, roughly, a year. The secretary of homeland security makes $175,000, but he is also on loan from the school to the government, which is paying nearly all his salary. Is that correct?

Mr. FORESMAN. Congressman, I will need to go back and—

Mr. DICKS. He is here today. He is here in the audience.

Mr. FORESMAN. I understand that. But in terms of the contractual relationship, I would like to provide you a written response to that so that we are very clear.

But on the first part of it, let me also acknowledge that when we talk about compensation packages, we have to remember that what my base salary is in the federal government, on top of it, there is a 33–34 percent package on top of it.

Mr. DICKS. Right.

Mr. FORESMAN. So I think part of it is looking at this in terms of the total compensation, but I am more than happy to provide a detailed written response to you.

Mr. DICKS. Now, as of January 2006, the national cybersecurity division had 27 government employees out of 40 full-time equivalent positions assigned. These 27 employees make up only 27 percent of the total workforce, with the remaining 73 percent being provided through contracts with one or more of 10 different private sector organizations, such as Booz Allen Hamilton and SRA International, Inc.

In addition, NCSD has contracts with Carnegie Mellon University totaling $19 million, which is one-fifth of the unit's total budget.

Now, that appears to me to be a very questionable practice. How can you have a person who is running the division and being paid by Carnegie Mellon also giving contracts to them of $19 million? I don't understand that.

Mr. FORESMAN. Congressman, three points on that. First, when I assumed this position in January, we did have a large number of unfilled positions, as well as a lot of contractors, IPAs and contract support.

We made a very deliberate policy decision in the department. That was the way to get the department up and running back when Congress created it.

But as we move forward, we are trying to transition as many positions as possible into full-time federal employee positions. That process continues to take time, but we have made hiring and filling vacant positions and transitioning as many from contract status to permanent status a priority.

In terms of Mr. Purdy and the relationship with Carnegie Mellon, we do have checks and balances in place. His ability to obligate funds is not sole and exclusive in the context of not having checks and balances.

And, in fact, what I will—

Mr. DICKS. What are the checks and balances?

Mr. FORESMAN. Well, there are a variety of checks and balances. You have to go through the business review process, through a procurement process.

And what I would like to do is describe those for you and for the committee in exact detail, because, Congressman, if I attempted to do it, I am going to miss an important part and that is going to create an incorrect picture and I want to paint the correct picture of what—

Mr. DICKS. Well, the picture isn't real pretty, as far as I am concerned. This doesn't look right to me.

Has he recused himself from making any decisions about Carnegie Mellon?

Mr. FORESMAN. Congressman, I believe in the context of his ethics agreement, he is, but, again, let me—

Mr. DICKS. He is right here. Why can't you let him testify?

Mr. FORESMAN. But, Congressman, he is not the witness and what I would prefer to do is to make sure that we get you a factual and accurate answer, please.

Mr. DICKS. Well, Mr. Chairman, I think the gentleman is here in the audience, I think we ought to have him testify.

Mr. LUNGREN. Well, the problem is he was not requested to testify. We did not notify that he was going to be asked to testify.

Mr. DICKS. Well, the administration's witnesses bring up people with them all the time, in all the hearings I have ever been in. If the person is there and can answer the question, I think the question ought to be answered.

Mr. LUNGREN. I don't want to avoid this, but that is not the procedure we follow in this subcommittee. We notice people. They are given an opportunity to know they are going to testify and if it is appropriate—

Mr. DICKS. How long is it going to take to get an answer to this question?

Mr. LUNGREN. Mr. Foresman, could you get an answer to us in written form within the week?

Mr. FORESMAN. Yes, sir. Well, what day of the week is it, Congressman, Wednesday?

Mr. LUNGREN. Yes.

Mr. FORESMAN. I think Friday is reasonable, yes, sir.

Mr. LUNGREN. And we will make that a part of the record, as well.

Ms. SANCHEZ. Will the gentleman yield?

Mr. DICKS. I yield.

Ms. SANCHEZ. I don't think it is going to be very difficult. I mean, this issue has been in the newspaper for about 6 months, almost day in and out in some of them. And I would imagine, Mr. Secretary, that you have this all written out already, because you have probably had to explain this over and over.

It is just that our committee hasn't really gotten the real explanation.

Mr. FORESMAN. Well, Congresswoman, I want to make sure that this committee, in terms of your oversight and responsibilities for our department and this particular area, that you get the information you need to do the job that you need to do.

So we will put posthaste on this when we get back to our offices today.

Mr. LUNGREN. So we will get that by Friday and we will make it a part of the record.

Mr. DICKS. Thank you, Mr. Chairman. I appreciate that.

Mr. LUNGREN. The gentleman's time—

Mr. DICKS. Well, let me just ask one final question.

Mr. LUNGREN. The only thing I just want to mention is Mr. Pearce hasn't asked any questions yet and we have a second panel coming up.

Mr. DICKS. Okay, that is fine. Thank you.

Mr. LUNGREN. Thank you.

Mr. Pearce is recognized for 5 minutes.

Mr. PEARCE. Thank you, Mr. Chairman.

Mr. Powner, over the course of time, GAO has issued you all some findings, recommendations to strengthen your ability to implement the cybersecurity and I just wonder which of the recommendations are considered a priority and where we stand on implementing those.

Mr. POWNER. My written statement today lays out recommendations in five broad areas and there are 25 specific recommendations in that statement. I would say the priority areas are in four key areas, threat assessments, vulnerability assessments and reduction efforts, bolstering analysis and warning capabilities, and putting in place recovery plans.

Mr. PEARCE. Mr. Foresman, the business roundtable report issued suggested that too many organizations, both public and private, had overlapping responsibilities in managing the Internet reconstitution.

Do you have any comment about their comment?

Mr. FORESMAN. Congressman, one of the first meetings I took when I became the undersecretary was 2 or 3 days after I arrived in Washington on the job, was to sit down with the business round-table and specifically to talk through a number of these issues.

You know, it is hard for any of us to assess whether there are too many or too few, but I think the one thing that is clear from the GAO report, one thing that is clear from our Cyberstorm exercise is we need to have clarity and coordination, increased clarity and increased coordination of roles and responsibilities.

We are far better than we were a year ago. There is still more work to be done. But, you know, I wouldn't assess whether we need more or fewer, but believe they need to be well coordinated.

Mr. PEARCE. Now, as I listened to Mr. Powner discuss the threat and vulnerability assessments, I wonder where we stand on accomplishing those.

Mr. FORESMAN. That is, Congressman, actually one of the things that will come out of the work of the sector coordinating council in developing the IT sector-specific plan, as we will do across all of the sectors.

Part of that will be the engagement of the public sector, the private sector, leveraging a wide array of U.S. government resources to do that vulnerability assessment, so that we understand what is it that we are trying to protect and how do we prioritize towards doing that.

And to that end, one thing I will just mention, Mr. Chairman, it may be worthwhile in the early part of January for us to come up and brief you on what is, in fact, in those sectors, what each of the sectors have come up with.

And the vulnerability analysis on the IT sector is one that I'm most anxious to receive.

Mr. PEARCE. Thank you, Mr. Chairman. I see my time is about expired.

Mr. LUNGREN. Does the gentlelady from Texas wish to participate in the second round?

Ms. JACKSON-LEE. Very briefly, Mr. Chairman, thank you.

I think I want to go back to my point of frustration, because we face daily challenges. And I want to ask or at least emphasize why I use the term frustration. It is because we have noted over the last couple of weeks the administration, and I will yield to their higher moral responsibility which has caused them to utilizes the extensive media that they have done, meaning the president has been making speeches almost every day, every other day, on the war on terror, which means that, I guess, there is a sense of urgency.

Of his public pronouncements, I don't see the equating of those public pronouncements with the agency that has the responsibility to carry forth those policies. So I find that particularly frustrating.

And I want to go to Mr. Powner. And you went rather quickly, excuse me for being redundant in asking the question, but I would like to hear those four points again. That was asked by the distinguished gentleman from New Mexico.

Then I would like you to categorize where we are, because those points that you enumerated were the key element of our line of homeland security defense, whether we are dealing with cybersecurity or we are talking about border patrol or protecting the borders.

And you have made, I guess, a limited assessment, but let me hear those again and, if you would, walk us through, so that we are awake, where we are in that, because that is my—again, I am using this word frustration—the urgency of getting this department back—not back, but on its feet in numerous areas, and we are now talking about cybersecurity, infrastructure of that.

And any number of incidences over the last couple of weeks show us that that is crucial. That is crucial.

Again, you gave us four points. Could you just—

Mr. POWNER. And, clearly, there are multiple ways to prioritize and I make these four comments because this is really the heart and soul of information security, whether it is our critical infrastructure or federal agencies or private sector organization security. But it starts with threat, understanding the threat.

Clearly, there has been a lot of work on threat. We have the U.S. CERT and there are many aspects within the department that work on threats. So it is not devoid of threat information. I think Mr. Foresman mentioned the threat needs to be bolstered through greater intelligence information. That is one area that could greatly be improved.

I think when you look at the requirement, it calls for a national threat assessment. I don't think we have seen that yet.

Ms. JACKSON-LEE. No, we have been talking about that for 3 years. But I will let you skip on. I got the gist of that one.

Mr. POWNER. So that is threat. The second one is vulnerability assessments. Mr. Foresman referred to the sector-specific plans that come out.

I would imagine that some of those plans may get at vulnerability assessments. Some of those plans likely may call for vulnerability assessments. Hopefully, we get vulnerability assessments within those plans at the end of the year.

The third area is looking at analysis and warning capability.

Ms. JACKSON-LEE. Analysis.

Mr. POWNER. And warning capability. And this is a point that I mentioned earlier, where the U.S. CERT, there is certain analysis and warning capability that currently exists, where we provide information on—more of it is after-the-fact type of vulnerabilities and incidents.

We need to get more on the front end with our analytical capabilities, where we get precursors to attacks. And I think the department acknowledges that and is working on that.

The fourth area then is recovery plans. We just completed a large review focusing on this, not only do the individual sectors need a recovery plan, and that is called for, but if you take the Internet, an Internet recovery plan is called for in national policy.

That doesn't exist to date. That is very important that we work in the government with the private sector in recovering the Internet, if, in fact, there is a large-scale outage. And I think some of those lessons learned from Katrina and 9/11 really drove that home.

Now, that wasn't a cyber event, but in terms of the partnering and working together to restore some things, there were many lessons learned from that.

Ms. JACKSON-LEE. Many lessons, many lessons. Mr. Chairman, I would, in conclusion—thank you very much, Mr. Powner—say that it is time for Secretary Chertoff to come again before this committee, the full committee, because I think there are some large vulnerabilities.

The idea that a threat assessment still may not be complete is one that I think should disturb this committee, Republicans and Democrats alike.

So I thank you, Mr. Powner and Mr. Foresman, for your testimony and your service.

I yield back.

Mr. LUNGREN. I thank the gentlelady. And I want to thank both witnesses for their testimony and responses to our questions.

Mr. Foresman, I know you are a busy individual, but perhaps you or some members of your staff could stay around to listen to what the other panel has to say, as we try to build that trust further.

Again, thank both of you for appearing. We appreciate it.

The chair would not like to call the second panel. Mr. William Pelgrin, Mr. Paul Kurtz, Mr. Guy Copeland, Mr. David Barron.

We have someone to the rescue who is going to try and bring the heat down a little bit here.

I thank the four of you for being with us. I introduced the individuals briefly beforehand and we would now ask the panel, again, gentlemen, your prepared testimony will be made a part of the record in its entirety, and we would ask you to please summarize your testimony.

And we will go from my left to right or your right to left, starting with Mr. William Pelgrin, director of the New York State Office of Cybersecurity and Critical Infrastructure Coordination.

STATEMENT OF WILLIAM PELGRIN, DIRECTOR, NEW YORK STATE OFFICE OF CYBER SECURITY AND CRITICAL INFRASTRUCTURE

Mr. PELGRIN. Good afternoon, Chairman Lungren, Ranking Member Sanchez, and distinguished members of the subcommittee. I am William Pelgrin, the director of New York State's Office of Cybersecurity and chair of the multi-state Information Sharing and Analysis Center.

I am honored to represent New York state and the multi-state ISAC to discuss our efforts to be more vigilant, prepared and resilient regarding cybersecurity.

Two days ago, we marked the fifth anniversary of the tragic event of September 11. Since 2001, much has been implemented to improve our nation's security posture. I am very proud of what has been accomplished in cybersecurity at both the New York state and multi-state levels.

Our achievements could not have been done without the support at the highest levels. In New York, Governor Pataki has been a true champion on these issues. And I would also like to thank Undersecretary Foresman. His leadership and support of our efforts are very much appreciated. It has been a great partnership with DHS and one that I believe has made a difference.

But we cannot be complacent. We need to stay one step ahead of those who wish to do us harm. More than ever, we must continue to make significant progress in our fight against cyber threats.

It is critical that we learn from the past in order to improve the future. It is not about how good we are, but about how good we can be. Cybersecurity is more about the management of technology. The best technology in the world, if it is not managed properly, can leave us vulnerable.

Our successes have been driven by the following guiding principles. It is not about one person or entity, it is about the collective effort. It can't be territorial. We have got to work together across sectors and geographic boundaries.

Trust must be earned. It is not a right. We have worked hard to earn trust. The culture must change. Implementing sound cybersecurity practices must be as second nature as buckling a seatbelt. This can only be done through education and awareness.

We must be deliverable oriented. The time to talk is over. It is the time to do.

My approach has been threefold. First, we wanted to make sure that New York state is strategically aligned to meet the emerging threats. My office was created in order to have an entity with a single focus, dedicated to addressing the highly specialized need of cybersecurity, one that wouldn't be diverted to other competing priorities.

Second, we recognized early on that we could not do this alone. So we focus on developing strong collaboration with others, true partnerships. We established the New York state public-private cybersecurity workgroup in 2002 to foster sharing across sector borders and to build important trust relationships.

The workgroup comprises high level executives from the public and private sectors, representing critical industries, including telecommunications, financial, utilities, chemical, health and food.

Third, we recognize that the traditional geographic borders are irrelevant when dealing with cybersecurity issues. So there was a need for strong partnerships with other states and local governments across the nation, as well as with our federal and international partners.

The multi-state ISAC was created in 2003 and I am pleased to say that all 50 states and D.C. are members. The mission of the MSISAC, consistent with the objectives of the national strategy to secure cyberspace, is to provide a common mechanism for raising the level of cybersecurity readiness and response in each state and with local governments.

This volunteering and collaborative effort provides a central resource for gathering information on cyber threats and events, providing two-way sharing of information between and among states, and with local governments, as well as with the federal government.

A key component of the MSISAC is our 7-by–24 cybersecurity center. This center provides cybersecurity monitoring for analysis of intrusions and other anomalous cyber activities for all the members of the multi-state ISAC.

The center works very closely with U.S. CERT, other cyber researchers, security vendors, and the ISPs. In addition, we have deployed equipment that provides real-time monitoring of network traffic, specifically to two states, one in New York and, most recently, Alaska.

Many other states and local governments have expressed an interest in being part of this service. The concept is that the collective view is more valuable and informative than a singular view.

Another key initiative is our cybersecurity alert map, which allows each state to identify and display its current cybersecurity status and contact information. I am pleased that all 50 states and D.C. have adopted this common cyber alert protocol.

What a tremendous step forward in facilitating information sharing than situational awareness.

We have a number of other initiatives focused on helping local governments address cybersecurity. They are facing the same issues that the states are. However, many of them don't have the necessary resources or expertise for the cyber challenges that they face.

For example, when we issued a cybersecurity advisory recommending patching vulnerable systems, I received a call from a town supervisor, telling me, "Will, I don't understand what you mean by patching. When I hear the word, I look for duct tape."

To aid local governments, we have established a local government cybersecurity committee, with representatives from towns, counties, cities, schools and state governments. The committee has developed a roadmap for addressing the cybersecurity needs of local governments.

In partnership with DHS, we have completed our first major deliverable, the first national cybersecurity guide for localities. It is called "Just Get Started," and I do have copies for the chairman and members of the committee, as well.

The goal of the guide was to keep it short, easy to read, like a magazine, that there would be periodic installments.

In closing, I have briefly highlighted for you some of our major accomplishments. The key guiding principle that has been instrumental in these efforts is collaboration. We must ensure that all stakeholders are at the table. We also need to realize that you can't get from A to Z overnight. You have to prioritize and move strategically.

I appreciate the opportunity to testify today and thank you, Chairman Lungren and the members of the subcommittee, for your strong leadership and attention to this important matter of cybersecurity.

Thank you.

[The statement of Mr. Pelgrin follows:]

PREPARED STATEMENT OF WILLIAM F. PELGRIN

Good Afternoon Chairman Lungren, Ranking Member Sanchez, and distinguished Members of the Subcommittee on Economic Security, Infrastructure Protection, and Cyber Security. I am William Pelgrin, the Director of New York State Office of Cyber Security and Critical Infrastructure Coordination and Chair of the Multi-State Information Sharing and Analysis Center (Multi-State ISAC).

I am honored to represent New York State and the Multi-State ISAC to discuss the challenges, successes and lessons learned in our efforts to address cyber security.

It is time for plain speaking—we must be open to sharing information. We must learn from the past to improve the future. Cyber security must be everyone's responsibility. I have adopted this mantra as a call to action.

Two days ago, we commemorated the 5th anniversary of the tragic events of September 11. Since 2001, much has been implemented to improve our nation's security posture. I am very proud of what has been accomplished in cyber security at both the New York State and Multi-State levels to assist in this effort to be more vigilant, prepared and resilient. But we cannot be complacent; we still have a long way to go.

Why We Must Be So Concerned?
- Cyber terrorism or human error can both have devastating consequences;
- Cyber attacks can originate from anywhere;
- The technology to launch such cyber attacks is relatively inexpensive and widely available; and
- Sophisticated computer expertise is no longer necessary to launch attacks.

My testimony today will describe our approach to address these issues and how we are working to improve the cyber security posture not only of New York State but of all the states and local governments in our nation. This could not have been done without the strong leadership of Governor Pataki, who has been a true champion of these issues.

Since it is the start that stops most of us, we took the approach of "let's just get started" using the "build it as you go" and "best effort" rules to move forward as quickly as possible.

The time to talk is over—it is the time for action.

For many it is very difficult to fully grasp the cyber challenges and threats that we face today. My method is to make it real and tangible in order to provide clarity and understanding of these issues.

None of us is as smart as all of us. Therefore, collaboration, cooperation and communication are the cornerstones of our approach. We can't do this alone. Our partnership with U.S. Department of Homeland Security has been a positive example of what can be accomplished when we truly work together toward a common goal.

Cyber security is more about management than technology. The best technology in the world, if not managed properly, with appropriate policies and procedures, will leave us vulnerable. We all must become champions for good cyber security practices and set an example for others to follow.

I would like to start off by describing my philosophy. I believe these guiding principles are major factors for our successes in New York, as well as with the Multi-State.
- First and foremost, it is not about one person or entity; it is about the collective effort.
- It is about moving in a common direction.
- Trust must be earned; it is not a right. We work hard to earn that trust.
- We have a willingness to share as much as possible without concern for what would or would not be shared with us. Over time, sharing is becoming two-way.
- The culture must change. Implementing sound cyber security practices must be as second nature as buckling a seatbelt.
- We continually strive to eliminate traditional bureaucratic impediments.
- We have created a safe haven in order to facilitate true collaboration and sharing.

The remainder of this testimony will describe how we addressed our challenges. First, we needed to strategically realign our focus to meet the emerging threats.

Creation of the New York State Office of Cyber Security and Critical Infrastructure Coordination

The New York State Office of Cyber Security and Critical Infrastructure Coordination (CSCIC) was established in September 2002 by Governor George E. Pataki in order to have an entity with a single focus dedicated to addressing the highly specialized needs of cyber security and critical infrastructure coordination.

The Office is responsible for leading and coordinating New York State's efforts regarding cyber readiness and resilience; expanding the capabilities of the State's cyber incident response team; monitoring the State's networks for malicious cyber activities; coordinating the process by which State critical infrastructure data is collected and maintained; as well as leading and coordinating geographic information technologies.

Second, we focused on developing strong collaboration with the private sector.

NYS Public/Private Sector Cyber Security Workgroup

Because more than 85% of critical infrastructure is owned or controlled by the private sector, we immediately saw the need to create true partnerships. New York State actively engaged the private sector in addressing the State's cyber security and critical infrastructure needs.

Our NYS Public/Private Sector Cyber Security Workgroup comprises private sector high-level executives and public sector commissioners to represent critical industry sectors, including telecommunications, financial and economic, utilities, public safety, chemical, health, food and education/awareness. For example, for the Telecommunications Sector, we have as co-chair from the private sector, the Vice President and Chief Cyber Security Officer for AT& T, and for the public sector, the Chair of the NYS Public Service Commission.

The Workgroup is examining the current state of cyber readiness throughout the entities within each sector, working to identify and assess vulnerabilities and identify mitigation strategies.

The Workgroup has published two reports: *Cyber Security: Protecting New York State's Critical Infrastructure* details the on-going efforts in New York State to address cyber security readiness and response, in both the public and the private sectors; and The *Best Practice Guidelines for Cyber Security Awareness* which includes a number of useful tips and practical advice, along with links to additional information for all New Yorkers on how to become more "cyber security aware."

The Workgroup has expanded its participation to include all major entities within the sectors. These entities work closely with the established sector chairs and New York State to more fully engage those critical entities to share information and build important communication relationships.

The Workgroup meets monthly via conference call with each sector and meets together as a full group in person periodically. The participation in this Workgroup has been tremendous, and the information sharing relationship with the private sector serves to better prepare and protect New York State. This mutual information sharing arrangement is an important component in helping to ensure the readiness and resilience of New York State's critical infrastructure assets—both public and private. We are truly breaking down the traditional barriers that have prevented the public and private sectors from communicating. This Workgroup is important not only to New York, but the nation as well.

We are also working collaboratively on the national level with the private sector, through the National ISAC Council. The Council represents the critical industry sectors and focuses on advancing the physical and cyber security of the critical infrastructures of North America. I'm honored to have been elected to serve as Vice Chair of the ISAC Council. This is another great example of strong relationships between the public and private sectors.

Third, we recognized that traditional geographic borders are irrelevant when dealing with cyber security issues, so the need was clear for strong partnerships with other states and local governments across the nation.

Multi-State Information Sharing and Analysis Center (Multi-State ISAC)

The Multi-State ISAC is a voluntary and collaborative organization. I am pleased to say that we have 50 states and the District of Columbia as members, and we are actively pursuing local governments and territories. The mission of the Multi-State ISAC, consistent with the objectives of the *National Strategy to Secure Cyberspace,* is to provide a common mechanism for raising the level of cyber security readiness and response in each state and with local governments. The MS–ISAC provides a central resource for gathering information on cyber threats to critical infrastructure from the states and providing two-way sharing of information between and among the states and with local government.

The U.S. Department of Homeland Security has officially recognized the Multi-State ISAC as the national ISAC for the states and local governments to help coordinate cyber readiness and response.

Major Objectives of the Multi-State ISAC

- to provide two-way sharing of information on cyber critical infrastructure incidents and threats
- to provide a process for gathering and disseminating information on cyber and physical threats to cyber critical infrastructures
- to share security incident information among critical industry sectors
- to focus on the cyber and physical vigilance, readiness, and resilience of our country's cyber critical infrastructure assets
- to promote awareness of the interdependencies between cyber and physical critical infrastructure as well as between and among the different sectors
- to ensure that all necessary parties are vested partners in this effort

• to work collaboratively with the public and private sectors to foster communication and coordination
• to coordinate training and awareness

The following major initiatives reflect the successes we—ve accomplished at both the New York State level and the Multi-State ISAC level.

7x 24 Cyber Security Center

One of the key components in addressing our cyber security needs is the establishment of a 7x24 cyber security center. This Center provides cyber security monitoring for and analysis of intrusions and other anomalous cyber activity for New York State agencies and public universities, as well as the members of the Multi-State ISAC. The State has deployed Intrusion Detection/Prevention Systems (IDS/IPS) for the State agencies. Since the inception of the IDS/IPS program in May 2003, more than 17 billion log entries have been analyzed. Currently we also provide intrusion prevention monitoring for the State of Alaska, and several other states are actively engaging the MS–ISAC in considering similar arrangements.

The Center monitors cyber intelligence activity at a State, national and global level. It works closely with US–CERT, cyber researchers, security vendors and ISPs. The Center distributes cyber security advisories and alerts to all New York State agencies, to members of the private sector through its Public/Private Sector Workgroup and to other States and local governments through the Multi-State ISAC. New York State also posts cyber alerts and advisories on its public website: *www.cscic.state.ny.us,* and the Multi-State ISAC through its public website: *www.msisac.org.*

The Center monitors State and local government websites for web page defacements and affected entities are notified. In 2005, 1,169 defacements have been reported out to state and local governments.

Incident Response Team

New York State has an incident response team to respond to cyber incidents. A mandatory incident policy has been issued to all state agencies, which outlines what must be reported and how. The goal of this policy is to ensure that a state entity recovers from an incident in a timely and secure manner and to minimize impact. Reporting incidents to a central group promotes collaboration and information sharing with other sites that may be experiencing similar problems.

The Multi-State ISAC Members also report incidents to the Multi-State ISAC. The Multi-State ISAC serves as the liaison between the states and US CERT for cyber incident reporting.

Multi-State ISAC Secure Portal and Cyber Security Alert Map

The Multi-State ISAC uses the US–CERT portal as its secure portal. The Multi-State ISAC's compartment on this portal serves as a central repository for Multi-State ISAC members to utilize as a secure mechanism in sharing important, secure and vital information among the states. The portal allows for secure emailing and includes a library so that Multi-State ISAC members can readily share information and documents, such as statewide policies, procedures, and white papers.

One of the most unique features on the Multi-State ISAC secure portal is an alert map application that the Multi-State ISAC developed. This is a map of the nation, in which each state displays its current cyber security alert level, along with contact information for the Multi-ISAC Members. The Multi-State ISAC members have adopted this common Cyber Alert Indicator Protocol process; thus, when any Multi-State ISAC member state is at a "Guarded" level for cyber, for example, all of the other Multi-State ISAC Members will know the specific criteria used to arrive at that level.

State ISACs on the Secure Portal

A major step in fostering the strong relationships between and among state and local governments is the build-out of the secure portal so that each MS–ISAC Member state will have its own section of the portal in which to communicate securely, share documents, and display alert level status. This pilot is currently underway with five states.

These individual state "ISACs" will include representatives from state agencies, counties, cities and other municipalities and educational institutions and will provide the following benefits to members:
• direct access to cyber security threat information from the State
• access to security awareness materials, including computer-based training modules
• access to security policy templates
• access to security-related solutions

- periodic meetings, teleconferences and webcasts to promote peer networking and information sharing

This initiative is focusing on building strong relationships between and among the state and local government entities to best ensure our cyber readiness.

To view examples of the alert map and the individual state ISAC sections of the portal, please refer to Appendix A.

Local Government Committee

Local governments face the same cyber security issues. However, many of them can be at a disadvantage in addressing the issues due to lack of resources and expertise. We are cognizant of the need for local government involvement and want local government as vested partners as we move forward.

To that end, I've established a Local Government Cyber Security Committee (Committee), with representatives from towns, counties, cities, and schools and state government. The Committee, established in May 2005, has been meeting monthly to develop a roadmap for addressing the cyber security needs of local governments. The Committee is focused on ascertaining the issues, building communication channels, and identifying mitigation strategies.

The Committee's goal was to develop a document that provides a non-technical resource to executives and managers to help them better understand the importance of cyber security and what they need to know about the issues.

The Committee has produced one of its first priority projects: the *Local Government Information Security: Getting Started Guide.* This is a brief, practical reference intended for entities that may not have the technology or information security expertise of other entities and therefore need a basic "how to get started" resource for addressing information security challenges.

This Guide is a joint effort with the U.S. Department of Homeland Security's National Cyber Security Division.

The Getting Started guide covers the following topics:
- Introduction to Information Security
- Why is Information Security Important
- What is an Unprotected Computer
- What is a Cyber Incident
- Top Ten Things that must be done
- Glossary of information security terms
- Daily/weekly/monthly/annual checklist for the designated information security individual(s)

Future volumes of the Guide will include appendices that expand on the topics presented in the first volume, providing more detail about the steps necessary to secure the information which the citizens have entrusted to local governments. The appendices will be distributed in installments periodically over the year and will contain non-technical, plain language descriptions with specific action steps, along with references for further information.

We are also working on compiling a national database of contact information for local government representatives so that we can communicate more effectively and share information, including cyber alerts and advisories, future appendices of the Guides and other relevant information.

National Webcast Initiative

The MS–ISAC, in cooperation with the U.S Department of Homeland Security, through its National Cyber Security Division, has launched a partnership to deliver a series of national webcasts which examine critical and timely cyber security issues.

Embracing the concept that "cyber security is everyone's responsibility," these webcasts are available to a broad audience to help raise awareness and knowledge levels. The webcasts provide practical information and advice that users can apply immediately. All sessions are recorded and archived for viewing via the MS–ISAC public website.

Thousands of individuals from across the country and around the world participate in the webcasts.

One of the highlights of the webcast program is the national webcast held in October as part of National Cyber Security Awareness Month. This webcast is focused on how to keep our children safe online and features an interactive play for 4th and 5th grade age levels. The session will be broadcast live via the Internet and satellite and will be rebroadcast several times throughout the day to maximize viewing in each time zone. Last October, more than 5,000 teachers, parents, students and others participated in that broadcast and we look forward to another successful event this October 4!

To view a listing of all webcasts conducted through the National Webcast Initiative, please refer to Appendix B.

Partnership with U.S. Department of Homeland Security, National Cyber Security Division

As highlighted in this testimony, the Multi-State ISAC has a strong partnership with the National Cyber Security Division (NCSD) and its operational arm, the US–CERT. Through this partnership, we work together on many initiatives including sharing and analyzing information regarding cyber threats and events, conducting national webcasts, publishing cyber security awareness materials, conducting cyber exercises, as well as National Cyber Security Awareness Month activities. These initiatives help further the goal of improving our nation's cyber security posture.

Training and Awareness Activities

In New York, we have a number of ongoing training and awareness activities including:

• *Annual Statewide Cyber Security Conference.* We just held our ninth annual Cyber Security Conference. This Conference is free of charge to government employees. Consistent with our motto that "Cyber Security is everyone's responsibility," the scope of the Conference has expanded over the years to where we now provide multiple tracks covering a wide spectrum of cyber security issues, including technical, legal, auditing, academia, business managers and local government. This is the largest free government conference of its type in the country.

• *Annual Kids Safe Online Conference.* We are sponsoring our second annual Kids Safe Online Conference next month. Our target audience includes parents, educators, law enforcement officers as well as kids. The subject is not only what are the dangers for children online, but what are the solutions. This Conference is free to the public.

• *Information Security Officers (ISOs).* New York was the first state to appoint a statewide Information Security Office and I believe the first to require each agency to appoint an information security officer. The agency ISOs have a dotted line reporting relationship with my Office. We hold monthly meetings with the ISOs where we focus on current issues and training opportunities. Agency ISOs are required to have twenty-four hours a year of continuing professional education. We also sponsor statewide cyber security training for ISOs and technical staff. For example, we are currently sponsoring a seven-week online course for information security professionals to increase their skills.

• *Technical Staff.* We are sponsoring training on secure coding for application developers. In the past, we provided a 12 week course designed to increase the cyber security knowledge of technical staff and prepare staff to sit for the CISSP (Certificated Information Security Systems Professional) Exam. This training was video taped and made available to state and local governments on a national level.

• *Senior Staff.* Once a year, we provide a half-day awareness session for agency heads and their senior staff. The focus is to keep them informed of cyber security issues and to ensure they have the requisite knowledge to address them. It's also important to employ unique and creative solutions to increase awareness and education. We need to make it real. One of the approaches I took was to demonstrate to agency commissioners what is really meant when a computer is hacked. By having them see first-hand what could happen, it increased their awareness of the importance of cyber security.

• *End Users.* We developed a toolkit for State agencies, along the same line as the toolkit developed for the Multi-State ISAC. This includes calendars, mouse pads and posters, all with the cyber security message. We also produced a cyber security video that is used for training new employees at State agencies, as well as local governments. This was also made available to state and local governments on a national level. In addition, we conducted a "phishing exercise" with several state agencies to assess the current state of cyber awareness and identify where further education is necessary.

• *Cyber Exercises.* We sponsor and participate in periodic cyber security exercises to test our plans, policies, practices and procedures.

In our role as Coordinator of the Multi-State Information Sharing and Analysis Center, we work with states to develop, share and collaborate on training and awareness activities including:

• *Proclamations:* In 2005, thirty-six Multi-State ISAC members reported that proclamations were issued by their respective governors proclaiming October 2005 as Cyber Security Awareness month. This is an increase of twenty-four from the previous year. This demonstrates the increasing awareness of cyber security issues at the state level. A copy of our 2005 Cyber Security Month After-Action Report is attached.

• *Tool Kits.* We develop an annual tool kit for the states to use to promote Cyber Security Awareness. This includes posters, calendars, mouse pads and new for 2006 is the development of Public Service Announcements that are customized for each state.

• *Cyber Exercise.* In partnership with U.S. Department of Homeland Security, we coordinate Multi-State (state and local government) participation in regional and national exercises to test our plans, policies, practices and processes in responding to a cyber event. We need to insure that we have the capability to provide prompt and accurate situational awareness reports at the state and national level.

• *Technical Training.* We coordinate state participation of state and local governments in national training programs sponsored by the federal government. We also negotiate some volume discounts for states to participate in training provided by the private sector.

• *End User.* We are just completing the development of a Computer Based Training Program that will be made available to state and local governments nationally. This is a tutorial which educates end users on the basics of information security and what their responsibilities are to safeguard our government information systems. We publish a monthly Cyber Security Newsletter for end users. The newsletter focuses on one cyber security issue each month that is relevant for end users/home users. The newsletter is distributed to the states and local government which then push it out to the end users.

For a summary of the MS–ISAC Accomplishments, please refer to Appendix C.

Funding for the Multi-State ISAC

We very much appreciate the fiscal support from the Department of Homeland Security for the Multi-State ISAC. The current funding level of one million dollars a year amounts to twenty thousand dollars per state. While we have worked hard to leverage this available funding, more meaningful, long lasting change would be possible if more funding was available. Our ability to help raise the awareness and preparedness of states and local governments (for example, intrusion prevention monitoring and correlation of data) to help improve their cyber security posture is constrained due to the limited fiscal resources.

I appreciate the opportunity to testify today. Thank you Chairman Lungren and Members of this Subcommittee for your strong leadership and attention to this important matter.

Appendix A

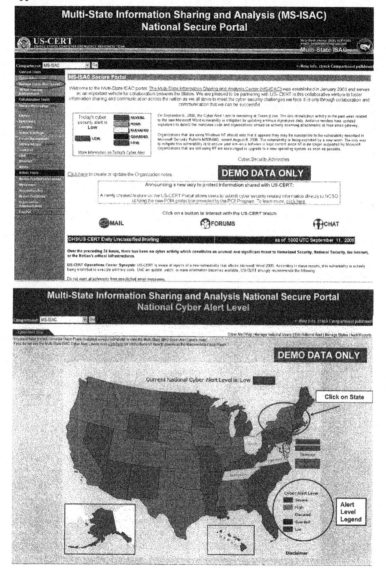

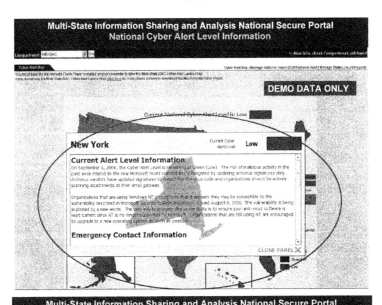

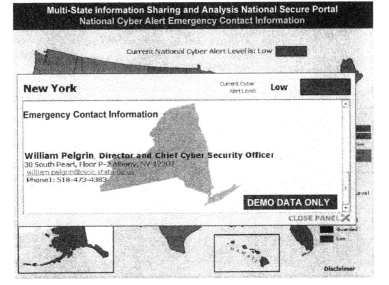

69

Multi-State Information Sharing and Analysis (MS-ISAC)
Secure Compartment Portal by State
Pilot Project: Pennsylvania, Florida, Michigan, Wisconsin, and New York

State of New York

State of Wisconsin

State of Pennsylvania

State of Florida

State of Michigan

Multi-State Information Sharing and Analysis (MS-ISAC)
Secure Compartment Portal by State
New York State

TODAY's CYBER SECURITY ALERT LEVEL

On September 6, 2006, the Cyber Alert Level is remaining at Green (Low). The risk of malicious activity in the past week related to the new Microsoft Word vulnerability is mitigated by updating antivirus signatures daily. Antivirus vendors have updated signatures to detect the malicious code and organizations should be actively scanning attachments at their email gateway.

Organizations that are using Windows NT should note that it appears they may be susceptible to the vulnerability described in Microsoft Security Bulletin MS06-040, issued August 8, 2006. The vulnerability is being exploited by a new worm. The only way to mitigate this vulnerability is to ensure your anti-virus software is kept current since NT is no longer supported by Microsoft. Organizations that are still using NT are encouraged to upgrade to a new operating system as soon as possible.

DEMO DATA ONLY

Today's cyber security alert is Low

Welcome to the NY- ISAC!

The New York State Information Sharing and Analysis Center (NY-ISAC) has been established to address the State of New York's cyber security readiness and critical infrastructure coordination. This initiative is led by William F. Pelgrin, Director, NYS Office of Cyber Security and Critical Infrastructure Coordination.

The mission of the NY-ISAC, consistent with the objectives of the National Strategy to Secure Cyberspace, is to provide a common mechanism for raising the level of cyber security readiness and response within the State of New York. The NY-ISAC provides a central resource for gathering information on cyber threats to critical infrastructure throughout the State and providing two-way sharing of information between and among state and local governments, educational institutions and emergency management entities.

Regardless of location, population or size, all entities face similar cyber security threats. These threats include identity theft, worms and viruses, loss of sensitive information, and other malicious activity. The vast amounts of information on cyber security can be overwhelming and the NY-ISAC and this portal will serve as a resource to assist in addressing the issues.

This portal is a joint effort between the State of New York and the Multi-State Information Sharing and Analysis Center (MS-ISAC). The MS-ISAC is a voluntary and collaborative organization comprising all 50 States and the District of Columbia focused on raising the cyber security readiness and response in each state.

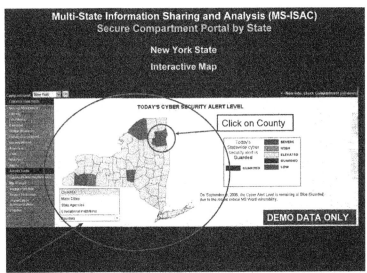

Drop Down Menu Selection By: Counties, Major Cities, State Agencies, and Educational Institutions

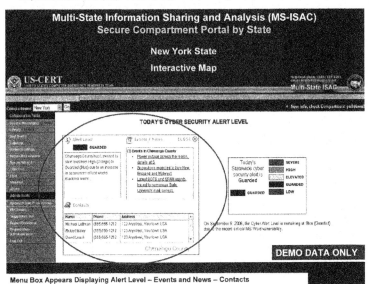

Menu Box Appears Displaying Alert Level – Events and News – Contacts

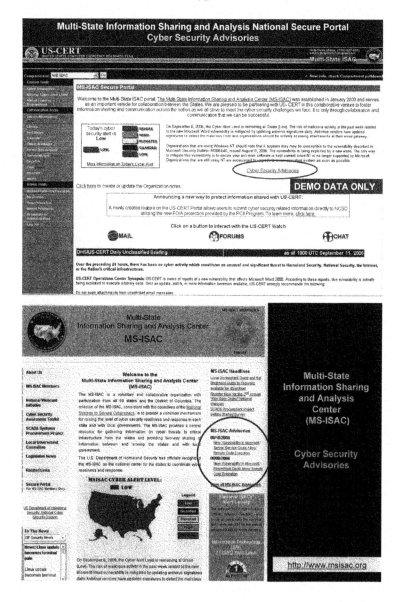

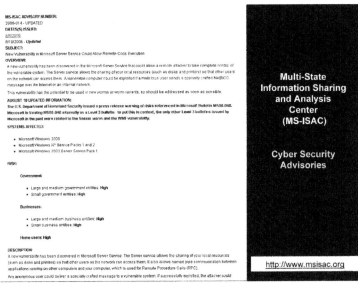

Appendix B—National Webcase Initiative Topics and Description
August 16, 2006
Instant Messaging

The broadcast presentation raised awareness on instant messaging (IM) and how IM is being used today as a source of communication online—both at home and at work. While IM can be a convenient and quick way to chat with others or collaborate on business matters, there are security concerns that we must understand and address. This webcast provided attendees with accurate and up-to-date information so that each of us can take the necessary steps to help protect ourselves online.

June 28, 2006
Remote Access

The broadcast presentation raised awareness on popular secure remote access solutions in terms of business use cases, high level deployment scenarios, and security and operational considerations.

April 13th, 2006
Voice-Over IP—How secure is your network infrastructure for handling VoIP?

VoIP is growing in popularity. Two-thirds of the world's 2,000 largest companies will be using VOIP systems in 2006 and by 2009, 27 million Americans will use Internet phones at home. The presentation raised awareness on network security issues and challenges that arise in today's network world.

February 16th, 2006
Identity Theft—The crime that keeps on taking!

The February 16th broadcast presentation focused on what ID Theft is, how to protect yourself, and what to do if you think you may have become a victim. The presenters walked through a variety of scenarios to help explain these concepts and provided specific advice on what steps to take.

December 15, 2005
Cyber Security Tips During the Holiday Season

The broadcast included such topics as online shopping transactions and the need to secure your private information online; understanding how to properly check your security settings on the new computer you just received as a gift; and what to look for when visiting legitimate web sites.

October 20, 2005
Protecting Our Children on the Internet

The National Webcast on Protecting Our Children on the Internet consisted of a play entitled Cyber Smart in Cyber Space geared toward the 4th and 5th grade age levels in which actors performed a cyber security-related skit interacting with the children. The play used content from *CyberSmart!*, an organization dedicated to teaching secure, responsible and effective Internet and computer use, and acted out with members of the *Plays for Living* organization, a nonprofit organization that utilizes live theater dramas to depict the real-life challenges and stresses many people face on a daily basis at work, at home and in the community.

July 20, 2005
Wireless Security

The webcast provided a non-technical presentation on Wireless Security. The webcast applied to all computer users—whether you are using your wireless-enabled laptop at the local coffee house or running a network that hosts sensitive customer data, you need to understand the issues and how to use wireless technology safely. Attendees walked away with a better understanding of the diversity of wireless devices that are used today, the security that can be applied behind the wireless network, and solutions of how you can be more secure.

May 18, 2005
Botnets

The webcast provided a non-technical presentation on BotNets. BotNets are becoming a significant problem across the Internet and are increasing at an alarming rate. They are a growing source for staging denial of service attacks, identity theft, phishing attacks and SPAM mail relay services. Please visit the archived presentation and learn about how to defend against BotNets, what to do when your machine has been compromised, and how to respond when your machine has been controlled by BotNets.

March 16, 2005
Are You Secure?. . .Are You Sure?
Vulnerability Management

The webcast provided a "low/medium technical" discussion about what each of us should do on a daily basis to be more secure. The volume of malicious cyber activity continues on an upward curve. The sophistication of hacker tools continues to grow while the expertise required to deploy them is decreasing. Phishing schemes are becoming increasingly difficult to discern from legitimate email. Botnets are increasing at an alarming rate. These facts require that your information systems are as secure as possible and that you have appropriate measures in place to decrease your vulnerability to these cyber threats.

February 9, 2005
Adware/Spyware:
How to Protect Yourself from Today's Most Dangerous Spyware Threats
The webcast provided a non-technical discussion about what each of us should do on a daily basis to be more secure. This session focused on an in-depth analysis of today's most egregious spyware/adware programs.

October 19 , 2004
Are YOU the Weakest Link?

The webcast provided a non-technical discussion about what each of us should do on a daily basis to be more secure. This session focused on the human elements of cyber security, which are just as important, if not more so, than the technical elements, and included examples of the various types of scams and pitfalls we need to watch out for, and how to protect ourselves.

August 26, 2004
Performing a Cyber Security Risk Assessment:
Why? When? and How?

The webcast focused on the steps organizations should take in addressing risk and provided timely and practical advice that can be applied immediately.

June 22, 2004
Cyber Security: The Three Things You Should Have Done Yesterday and The Three Things You Should Do Today

The webcast included discussion of the biggest challenges to security, what you should have already been doing in your organization to address those challenges, and what you must do today.

Appendix C—Highlights of MS–ISAC Accomplishments
- establishment of a 24 x 7 operations center
- distribution of cyber security advisories and bulletins
- cyber incident response assistance to MS–ISAC Members
- monthly Member conference calls
- annual meetings of the Members
- two MS–ISAC websites—a public and a secure website
- participation in cyber exercises, including the national Live Wire and Cyber Storm exercises
- development and adoption of common cyber alert level protocols
- development of draft cyber incident reporting protocols
- support and promotion of National Cyber Security Awareness Month
    MS–ISAC Deliverables for 2005 National Cyber Awareness Month:
       36 MS–ISAC Members (35 States and the District of Columbia) signed proclamations recognizing Awareness Month;
       Cyber Security Toolkits were developed and distributed to all 50 States and the District of Columbia;
       PSAs for Governors were distributed;
       National Webcast was conducted with more than 5,000 registrants from across the country.
       Awareness Month materials available at: *http://www.cscic.state.ny.us/msisac/ncsa/oct05/index.htm*
- development and execution of legal NDA for the Members to sign
- development and adoption of the MS–ISAC Business Plan
- development and adoption of the MS–ISAC Charter
- development and adoption of MS–ISAC Member Representative Guidelines
- development and adoption of ISAC Council Representation Guidelines
- development and adoption of MS–ISAC Contact Administration Guidelines
- establishment of the MS–ISAC Nominating Committee
- issuance of white papers
- served as chair for the state and local section of the "Awareness and Outreach" Task Force of the NCSP—the Task Force issued a report detailing specific action items to be taken to increase end user cyber security awareness
- collaboration with all necessary parties

Mr. LUNGREN. Thank you very much.

Now, we will hear from Mr. Paul Kurtz, the executive director of the Cybersecurity Industry Alliance.

STATEMENT OF PAUL B. KURTZ, EXECUTIVE DIRECTOR, CYBER SECURITY INDUSTRY ALLIANCE

Mr. KURTZ. Mr. Chairman and other members of the committee, thank you very much for asking me here today.

Cyber systems are our newest and most pervasive infrastructure. They drive and organize every fact of our collective and individual lives from national and economic security to personal health and wellbeing.

And, yet, we do not have a strategic national capability to assess how well the mot critical systems are protected and what the consequences are if they fail. There is little strategic direction or leadership from the federal government in the area of information security.

Ensuring resiliency and integrity of our information infrastructure and protecting the privacy of our citizens should be a higher priority for the government. We must move beyond philosophy and statements of aspiration to defining priorities and programs.

CSIA believes the government has a responsibility to lead, set priorities and coordinate and facilitate protection and response.

Let me be clear. This is not a call for regulation for intervention. This is a call for leadership.

So if I could, I am going to depart from my prepared notes and list six recommendations for consideration for DHS.

Number one, lead, lead, lead. Number two, prevention and mitigation programs. In this area, I would highlight two key important points. R&D, Doug Bond, who is the head of cybersecurity R&D at DHS is doing a fantastic job, but he is lost in a bureaucratic morass. Doug's work needs to be recognized. It needs to be funded appropriately.

Second, in this area, we need to investigate incentives specifically facilitating the growth of insurance.

The third area that I would highlight would be establish an active early warning program that embraces the private sector. Currently, the ITISAC is being held at arm's distance by the Department of Homeland Security. It should be more fully embraced and its work should be recognized.

Fourth, we need to establish command and control procedures for when the balloon goes up, and it will go up. That means two key questions. A, what is the process for determining an incident of national significance? What agencies are involved inside the government? Who is involved in the private sector, as well?

Secondly, what are the implications of that decision? Legally, what does it mean for government? What does it mean for the private sector? A cyber incident of national significance, that language is drawn from the national response plan that has been prepared by DHS.

The fifth recommendation is ensure we have resilient communications in place to execute command and control when a crisis surfaces. So imagine when we have a problem, we are going to grab that phone or we are going to use the computer, but think of the phone in an IT environment.

Will it work when the very infrastructure is under attack? So we need to ensure we have resilient communications in place.

The sixth recommendation is to establish a national information assurance policy, which enshrine basically the five recommendations that I outlined before.

The protection of the information infrastructure goes beyond DHS. Clearly, the president has established that DHS has the lead in coordination. But when the balloon goes up and when we have problems, DOD will be involved, the FTC will be involved, and multiple other agencies will be involved at the same time.

And with that, I will close and I will take questions later.

Thank you.

[The statement of Mr. Kurtz follows:]

PREPARED STATEMENT OF PAUL B. KURTZ

Introduction

Chairman Lungren, Ranking Member Sanchez and members of the Subcommittee, thank you for the opportunity to testify today before the House Subcommittee on Economic Security, Infrastructure Protection, and Cybersecurity. My name is Paul Kurtz and I am Executive Director of the Cyber Security Industry Alliance (CSIA).

CSIA is the only advocacy group dedicated to ensuring the privacy, reliability and integrity of information systems through public policy, technology, education and awareness. The organization is led by CEOs from the world's top security providers who offer the technical expertise, depth and focus needed to encourage a better understanding of security issues. It is our belief that a comprehensive approach to ensuring the security and resilience of information systems is fundamental to global protection, national security and economic stability.

Before joining CSIA, I served at the White House on the National Security Council and Homeland Security Council. On the NSC, I served as Director of Counterterrorism and Senior Director of the Office of Cyberspace Security. On the HSC, I was Special Assistant to the President and Senior Director for Critical Infrastructure Protection.

My testimony will address four themes for consideration by Congress on refining the role of the Department of Homeland Security as it relates to national cyber security:

- Inadequate attention
- Lack of leadership
- No plan to prevent or minimize a major cyber disaster
- No plan for working with the private sector to recover from a cyber disaster

Cyber Security is Receiving Inadequate Attention from DHS

Last week in his updated national strategy for counterterrorism, President George W. Bush declared that "America is safer but we are not yet safe." The reality of physical terror occurring in the United States of America has riveted our attention since the attacks on September 11, 2001. Prevention of any physical incident of horror has since been priority one.

The President's reminder for vigilance clearly applies to threats against our physical well-being, but his admonition must also apply to the threats against cyber security. To some the idea of terrorists or hackers breaking into computers may sound like an abstract threat, especially when compared to the shock of a suicide bomber killing innocent people and destroying property. However, a successful massive cyber attack could trigger grave harm for many Americans if it knocked out communications and information systems for emergency response, energy, transportation, and other critical resources that depend on IT. The nation experienced such vivid fallout from a regionalized natural disaster last year in the aftermath of Hurricane Katrina—imagine this disaster on a national scale.

Since 9/11, responsibility for coordinating federal efforts on national safety shifted to the Department of Homeland Security. DHS has predictably reacted to a myriad of security challenges by focusing first on immediate physical threats. This focus is understandable, but it has also impeded progress toward stronger national cyber security. As a result, the United States remains unprepared to defend itself against a massive cyber attack or to systematically recover and reconstitute information systems after a successful attack.

My testimony will describe what DHS is and is not doing with respect to national cyber security, plus the need for DHS to specify how it and the private sector would coordinate actions if a massive cyber attack were to occur. By realistically refining the Department's role in national cyber security, DHS can escalate cyber security efforts in concert with efforts to prevent physical terror in America.

There is no leadership at DHS for national cyber security

Despite publication of more than 750 pages of strategies, directives and response plans, leadership in the U.S. government on cyber security is clearly absent. The practical significance of lack of leadership means the nation is not ready for a major disruption to our information infrastructure.

National coordination of cyber security is the purview of the Department of Homeland Security, and its related leadership position is Assistant Secretary for Cyber Security and Telecommunications. This new position was established in July 2005 by Secretary Chertoff specifically to elevate the importance of cyber security in relation to DHS's main focus on physical security. Unfortunately, fourteen months later, the Assistant Secretary position is unfilled, which reflects the low priority DHS still has toward cyber security. No one is in charge to lead efforts to protect information infrastructure against cyber attacks or to lead response and recovery.

Another consequence of this leadership vacuum at DHS is an unclear, uncoordinated strategy for cyber security. The agency has pushed plenty of paper on the topic but people responsible for securing information technology in government, public and the private sector would be hard pressed to identify the top DHS priorities.

The threats to information security are real. Digital systems underpin vital infrastructure throughout the nation and a major disruption to, or widespread lack of confidence in these systems could have a devastating effect on our citizens, our economy and security. The real need is for concrete action guided by a few key national priorities understood by those who must ensure cyber security. DHS needs to immediately fill the position for Assistant Secretary for Cyber Security and Telecommunications to crystallize a few key priorities, and develop programs that support and achieve those priorities.

An important role for the new Assistant Secretary will be ensuring that priorities for cyber security reflect the fact that all critical functions of all industry sectors rely on IT and telecommunications. Coordination and leadership should be the primary concern for DHS.

Lastly, DHS and the White House can take steps to consolidate multiple presidential-level advisory bodies in the area of IT and telecommunications. For example, we have NSTAC and NIAC that clearly have overlapping responsibilities and areas of inquiry. These should be combined to ensure that presidential advice and recommendations are made holistically, looking across key critical infrastructures, and not in separate silos.

DHS needs to specify steps to prevent and/or minimize a massive cyber attack or telecommunications disaster

DHS documents such as the *National Response Plan* and the *National Infrastructure Protection Plan* attempt to not omit any unconsidered detail. Virtually no agency, program or initiative is left unmentioned in sweeping surveys of the cyber security landscape. The downside to this ocean of detail is that every point seems equally important. Lack of prioritization makes it difficult for organizations to take practical coordinated action to secure their information systems.

CSIA believes this lack of prioritization dilutes the Department's limited resources and makes it less effective in preparing the nation against a massive attack. DHS should articulate a smaller set of priorities focused on preventing and/or minimizing the likelihood or severity of a massive cyber attack or telecommunications disaster.

Creating cyber security for critical systems entails using a combination of technological solutions and best practices for IT. With regard to cyber security technology, its successful use is linked to understanding vulnerabilities of operating systems, applications, networks, and literally thousands of protocols that enable modern IT. Acquiring this knowledge is a moving target due to the complex interdependencies of these technologies and their continuous evolution.

There are 4 major areas of logical activity that DHS should crystallize programs around:

- Risk Management—identification and classification of Critical Infrastructure
- Research & Development—solutions to identify, prevent and recover from attacks
- Incentives—encourage problems to be resolved, not postponed
- Insurance—ensures continuing US financial viability after a cyber loss

Risk Management

An important starting place is for DHS to encourage organizations to pursue cyber security as they would manage other types of risks. In evaluating the nation's IT resources, DHS should help identify the most critical interdependencies and urge organizations to concentrate on protecting those systems first. One positive effort underway is the partnership between DHS and the private sector in developing a protection plan for the IT infrastructure. Under the plan, the private sector is identifying common risk-management processes and techniques. However, this effort is lacking senior-level attention at DHS.

Research & Development

DHS could play a major national role by funding cyber security research and development (R&D) in the private sector. Instead, more than 98 percent of last year's $1.039 billion science and technology budget of DHS went to R&D on weapons of mass destruction. Less than 2% ($18 million) was for cyber security, and of that only about $1.5 million was for basic research.[1]

We understand the concern about threats to physical security, but CSIA believes DHS has inadvertently placed the nation in the way of another harmful vector by virtually ignoring R&D on cyber security.

Where DHS has spent money on cyber security R&D there has been some success. Over the past 18 months, the Department's Science and Technology (S&T) Directorate has participated in a technology demonstration project with the Oil and Gas sector. The project, entitled LOGIIC—Linking the Oil and Gas Industry to Improve Cybersecurity—is a public-private partnership between DHS, several companies from the oil and gas sector, process control system (PCS) and information security technology vendors, and the National Labs. This project is aimed at reducing vulnerabilities in process control environments used in the oil and gas sector by establishing a framework for assessing risks, evaluating new technologies, integrating these new technologies into a test environment, and demonstrating commercial

---

[1] See CSIA Policy Briefing, "Federal Funding for Cyber Security R&D" (July 2005).

event detection and correlation technologies that can significantly enhance situational awareness on PCS networks used in refineries and other large industrial facilities.

There is strong historical precedent for federally funding R&D for emerging technologies of national significance. The Internet is the most famous example, beginning with seed money in 1962 from with the Defense Advanced Research Projects Agency's (DARPA). The Internet is now a vital global infrastructure almost entirely owned and operated by the private sector. Other examples of federal funding for R&D that resulted in important innovations for cyber security include firewalls, intrusion detection systems, fault tolerant networks, open operating systems, cryptography and advanced authentication. CSIA urges DHS to shift a larger portion of its R&D budget to programs that will bolster national cyber security.

Incentives

The time-tested government practice of offering incentives for private investment is another avenue worthy of examination by DHS. By offering incentives such as tax credits for implementation of security solutions, the federal government could dramatically accelerate adoption of measures to shore up national cyber security—just as it has done to spur other initiatives deemed as important for the country by Congress. The key is to develop very carefully-crafted incentives targeted at high priority systems such as certain SCADA systems and Internet security protocols. Many SCADA systems operate on unsupported application platforms and must be moved to a virtual "sandbox" to remediate immediate and urgent security threats.

Insurance

On a related non-technical note, insurance is a practical way for organizations to recover from catastrophic loss. Private insurance policies, however, do not usually provide "cyber risk coverage" due to the newness of this concept and lack of data enabling insurers to establish actuarial loss tables and a viable premium structure. To be effective, premiums for cyber attack coverage would have to include natural risk management incentives for organizations to balance the cost of premiums against the cost of taking preventative measures for security. CSIA believes DHS, in partnership with the Department of Commerce, should sponsor research into viable uses of private-sector insurance coverage for cyber attacks.

DHS has not specified how it will work with the private sector to a cyber incident of national significance

The other major yet unarticulated priority for DHS is describing how it will work with the private sector to respond to and recover from a massive failure of information technology systems—whether from a cyber attack or a natural disaster. This issue is important because it's the private sector—not DHS—that owns and operates information technology systems for most of the nation's critical infrastructure. The unanswered question affecting all is: What is a suitable role for DHS as well as other key federal agencies, including DoD and the FCC in facilitating recovery and reconstitution from a cyber incident of national importance?

DHS is well aware that the private sector "runs the show," which may account for its encouragement of public-private partnerships. I am sure that everyone involved with the multitude of DHS-sponsored public-private partnerships participates with the best of intentions, but there is a lack of clarity in what this work is accomplishing. The Government Accounting Office recently reported that progress on those initiatives is limited, some lack time frames for completion, and relationships between these initiatives are unclear.[2]

Consequently, DHS needs to articulate a chain-of-command for each step of recovery and reconstitution. For example, the DHS's U.S. Computer Emergency Readiness Team (US–CERT) may be aware of a network attack, but the North American Network Operators Group (NANOG) is the operational forum for backbone/enterprise networking. Considerations for this type of situation include:
  • Which entity should be in charge of coordinating the actual work of recovery and reconstitution?
  • What, if any, related legal authority is possessed by DHS and the federal government?
  • What obligations do private sector entities have to obey directives from DHS?
  • Who would resolve conflicting demands for scarce cyber resources?
  • What enforcement power does DHS have in the process of helping the nation recover from a cyber disaster?

In this context, I would note that DHS in February sponsored "Cyber Storm," a large-scale exercise focused on some of these questions. CSIA and its members sup-

---

[2] "Challenges in Developing a Public/Private Recovery Plan," GAO–06–863T (July 28, 2006).

ported the exercise but some six months after the event, DHS's after action report containing lessons learned has not been shared with key owners and operators in the private sector.

In addition to chain-of-command, DHS needs to articulate an emergency communications system that works even when standard telecommunications and Internet connectivity are disrupted. Emergency communications entail more than simply establishing a resilient mechanism allowing people to talk. It also requires advance identification of the right people from appropriate organizations who speak the "same language" for establishing rapid recovery and reconstitution of national systems.

These are but a few of the details that must be articulated and agreed upon in advance if the nation is to truly prepare for recovery and reconstitution from a cyber disaster. Ostensibly, DHS would have a leading role in planning.

These issues should be answered in the DHS's 400-plus page *National Response Plan*. Unfortunately, the plan does not articulate clear answers on how federal agencies work with each other, with other government entities, or with the private sector in responding to a national disaster. Instead of one coordinator, there are at least six: Homeland Security Operations Center, National Response Coordination Center, Regional Response Coordination Center, Interagency Incident Management Group, Joint Field Office, and Principal Federal Official. The *National Response Plan's* discussion of cyber security is contained in the "Cyber Incident Annex." The Annex mentions many other federal departments and agencies with "coordinating" responsibility for cyber incident response, including Defense, Homeland Security, Justice, State, the Intelligence Community, Office of Science and Technology Policy, Office of Management and Budget, and State, Local, and Tribal Governments. The agency tasked with maintaining the *National Response Plan* is FEMA.

As I draw toward the end of my testimony, I wish to comment on one other topic that also requires close coordination of the government and private sector—namely, the need for a cyber early warning system that provides the nation with situational awareness of attacks. DHS has sponsored some mechanisms toward this end, such as US–CERT, and Information Sharing and Analysis Centers (ISACs) that share some cyber alert data from the private sector with the federal government. As noted by the Business Roundtable, however, the nation lacks formal "trip wires" that provide rapid, clear indication that an attack is under way.[3] This mechanism would be akin to NOAA's National Hurricane Center, which usually can provide a day or so of advance notice before a dangerous storm lands ashore. Cyber attacks often provide far less notice to prepare and react. DHS should lead the establishment of an efficient national cyber warning system because the private sector is most likely to first detect an attack, and data correlation and follow through coordination closely involves the government.

Summary of Recommendations

In summary, CSIA offers the following recommendations for the Subcommittee's consideration:

Increase Attention to Cyber Security. DHS has inadvertently exposed the nation to another vector of attack by providing inadequate attention to cyber security. The Department should carefully assess its priorities to achieve more balance by shifting some attention from an almost exclusive focus on physical security.

Appoint a Leader. There is no leader at DHS who is solely responsible for cyber security. DHS should swiftly fill the open position of Assistant Secretary for Cyber Security and Telecommunications to close the leadership vacuum.

Plan to Prevent or Minimize a Major Cyber Disaster. DHS is too preoccupied with appearing to be in control of every detail related to cyber security. DHS should shift this energy to articulating a smaller set of priorities focused on preventing and/or minimizing the likelihood or severity of a massive cyber attack or telecommunications disaster.

Plan to Work with the Private Sector to Recover from a Major Disaster. The existing DHS "plan" for recovery cites more than a dozen federal departments and agencies with "coordinating" responsibility—not including state, local and tribal governments. DHS needs to clearly articulate a chain-of-command between government and the private sector for recovery from a major cyber disaster.

---

[3] Business Roundtable, "Essential Steps to Strengthen America's Cyber Terrorism Preparedness" (June 2006); see also Section 15 of Homeland Security Presidential Directive 5, "Management of Domestic Incidents" (Feb. 28, 2003), and the *National Strategy to Secure Cyberspace* (Feb. 2003).

With that, I appreciate the opportunity to testify today and am pleased to answer your questions. Kurtz testimony before House Subcommittee on Economic Security, Infrastructure Protection, and Cybersecurity 9/13/2006

Information Assurance

Federal Agency Roles and Responsibilities Cycle

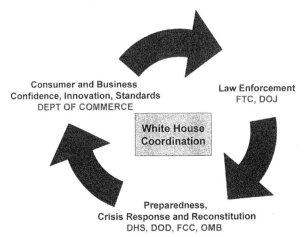

Mr. LUNGREN. Thank you very much for your testimony. I was trying to write as fast as I could, since you departed from your prepared text.

[Laughter.]

Mr. KURTZ. It is all in the written statement. I will put this together and send it.

Mr. LUNGREN. The chair recognizes Mr. Guy Copeland, the chairman of the Information Technology Sector Coordination Council.

STATEMENT OF GUY COPELAND, CHAIR, INFORMATION TECHNOLOGY SECTOR COORDINATING COUNCIL

Mr. COPELAND. Mr. Chairman, distinguished members of the subcommittee, thank you for inviting me here today.

As chairman of the Information Technology Sector Coordinating Council, I commend you for your attention to cyber and telecommunications security. I am also a vice president at Computer Sciences Corporation, but I am offering my personal reflections here today.

Five years ago this week, we suffered a devastating terrorist attack. 9/11 did not include a cyber attack component, but it reaffirmed how dependent we are on information technology and communications.

As an IT sector witness, I am focusing on our sector, but I also acknowledge the efforts of so many others who are dedicated to our common cause in their respective sectors.

The IT Sector Coordinating Council formally began in January 2006, with over 30 founding members. It is broadly representative of the sector and works with DHS, our sector-specific agency, the national cybersecurity division, or NCSD, and other organizations, in developing strategies and policies for critical infrastructure protection, collaborations, analysis and information sharing.

The IT sector's 5-year-old information sharing and analysis center, or ITISAC, is recognized and endorsed by the IT Sector Coordinating Council as our lead for the sector.

Under Secretary Foresman, Assistant Secretary Steffen, and Mr. Purdy have all worked tirelessly to include us in initiatives that affect the private sector. During and since its formation, the IT Sector Coordinating Council actively engage with government colleagues in the update of the national infrastructure protection plan, the NIPP, and we have formed a joint effort with them to draft the IT sector-specific plan.

Secretary Chertoff has proposed the establishment of an assistant secretary position, as you have discussed earlier. We stand ready to work with the new assistant secretary. We have not been on hold awaiting this appointment, but it is very important to us.

Recognizing the importance of IT and communications, Under Secretary Foresman, as he stated earlier, has recently directed his deputy undersecretary, Robert Zitz, to provide day-to-day oversight of the NCSD and the national communications system, which together constitute the cybersecurity and telecommunications organization.

I have some observations and suggestions. Trusted partnership is a key priority. DHS leadership has made huge strides to improving partnership, but still appears to be hampered by the application of laws and regulations rightly intended for the protection of a procurement or regulatory relationship, but not for the operational partnership that homeland security needs.

Adequate operational preparedness and timely response require physical collocation and daily interaction. DHS should build on its over 20 years experience of the national coordinating center for telecommunications, the NCC, add representatives from the IT sector and the other time critical or sometimes we call them the millisecond sectors, and resident members should represent the core group of each sector. That is, the most important entities for crisis response.

Ultimately, this should become the national crisis coordination center.

Since its establishment, the NCC has been collocated in the defense information systems agency headquarters, with the DOD's joint task force for global network operations. Current plans call for the NCC to relocate with the DHS U.S. CERT, as you heard earlier today.

Instead, DOD, DISA and DHS should consider collocating all of them, the U.S. CERT, the NCC, the JTFGNO, and perhaps other important elements. That will allow for maximum interaction leading to enhanced efficiency and value for both government and industry, for both homeland and national security missions.

Ultimately, the collocation facility could be a part of the national crisis coordination center.

Mr. Chairman, subcommittee members, Congress can help. In my written testimony, there are more details, but here, briefly, are a few recommendations.

Examine the collocation of those three entities, the NCC, the CERT and the JTFGNO, and other appropriate ones, to add better value. Examine the national crisis coordination center concept. Work with DHS and the IT Sector Coordinating Council and the Telecommunications Sector Coordinating Council to agree on cybersecurity priorities and ensure that DHS has the resources to implement them.

Create a better environment for the critical infrastructure protection partnership. Consider forming a bipartisan House caucus for cybersecurity for IT and communications, to help you all understand the issues and complexities better.

Encourage broader industry participation in critical infrastructure protection through membership in the sector coordinating councils and the ISACs.

Mr. Chairman, thank you again for inviting me to appear today.

[The statement of Mr. Copeland follows:]

PREPARED STATEMENT OF GUY L. COPELAND

Mr. Chairman, distinguished members of the Subcommittee, thank you for inviting me to testify before you this afternoon. On behalf of the members of the Information Technology Sector Coordinating Council, I commend you for your continuing attention to Cyber and Telecommunications Security.

Five years ago this week, we suffered the most devastating, terrorist attack in the history of our nation. The deliberate, horribly evil assaults on that day did not include a cyber attack. But they immediately reaffirmed how dependent we are on our information technology and communications sectors to respond quickly and effectively in any emergency and to recover and reconstitute normal societal functions. Subsequent analysis also showed that the technologies of these two sectors are equally crucial to prevention and preparedness at all levels.

A little over a year ago now, Katrina painfully reminded us that natural emergencies can be devastating. The scale of Katrina's impact and the response required was unprecedented. Once again though, communications and information technology were essential to response, recovery and reconstitution. Lessons learned have since been folded into the preparedness posture and emergency plans of the critical institutions, both industry and government.

My testimony today is based, in part, on my experiences and observations on how we have reacted to these and other tragedies. I've formed these observations, in part, based on my experience as Chairman of the Information Technology Sector Coordinating Council (IT SCC) and the immediate past President of the Information Technology Information Sharing and Analysis Center (IT-ISAC). Additionally, I am drawing on my experience as Vice President of Information Infrastructure Advisory Programs at Computer Sciences Corporation (CSC). However, I must emphasize that I am not speaking on behalf of CSC, the IT SCC or the IT-ISAC. I am offering my personal reflections, previously shared with key leaders in each organization.

We—both the Private Sector and Government—have been building an increasingly strong partnership, starting long before DHS was created. The level and sophistication of activities and initiatives has grown tremendously during that period. As the Information Technology sector witness today, I am focusing my comments in that sector. But I am equally proud of the efforts of my friends, colleagues and others who are equally dedicated to our common cause in their respective sectors. Many companies—large and small—are among our best citizens in terms of their selfless contributions.

IT SCC

In January 2005, while then serving as the President of the Information Technology Information Sharing and Analysis Center (IT–ISAC), I briefed a joint industry and government group on an initial proposal to begin an effort in the IT sector to consider the formation of the IT Sector Coordinating Council (IT SCC). Working with Mr. Harris Miller, President of ITAA, the leadership of the IT–ISAC and other sector leaders and with the facilitation assistance of Meridian Institute provided by DHS, we developed the necessary formation documents through 2005. In November 2005, we announced the interim IT SCC and in January 2006, the formal charter, first slate of officers and the executive committee were approved by over thirty founding members.

As with SCC's representing electricity, financial services, telecommunications, water, transportation, and others, the IT–SCC was organized to serve as a central point of coordination, collaboration and information sharing among the many members of the sector, and with the Federal agency(ies) responsible for interacting with a given private sector on critical infrastructure protection. The Department of Homeland Security—specifically the National Cyber Security Division (NCSD)—is the designated Sector Specific Agency responsible for collaborating with the IT sector.

In January, the IT–SCC completed its formation procedures, ratified its operating charter, and elected its leadership. With Harris's departure from ITAA, Greg Garcia, ITAA's Vice President for Information Security, was elected to the SCC' Executive Committee, as the Secretary. I was elected Chairman; Michael Aisenberg of VeriSign, Vice Chairman; and Larry Clinton of the Internet Security Alliance, Treasurer.

During and since its formation, the leadership and members of the IT SCC have been actively engaged in collaborative partnership with their government colleagues. We were invited to participate fully in the update of the National Infrastructure Protection Plan (NIPP) and our plans committee, under the leadership of Paul Kurtz of the Cyber Security Industry Alliance and John Lindquist of EWA, has formed a joint writing effort with our government colleagues, led by Cheri McGuire of the NCSD at DHS, to draft the IT Sector Specific Plan (SSP) which will in a few months be completed, staffed with our respective IT SCC and IT Government Coordinating Council membership, and approved as an annex to the NIPP. This joint effort exemplifies a marked improvement in the partnership as compared to the earliest days of DHS. The leadership on both sides should be commended for the strides that have been made.

IT sector leadership has been pleased with the relationships we have developed with the current leadership within DHS. In particular, Under Secretary for Preparedness, the Honorable George Foresman: Assistant Secretary for Infrastructure Protection, Mr. Robert Stephan, and Acting Director of the National Cyber Security Division, Mr. Donald "Andy" Purdy, have all worked tirelessly to include us in initiatives that affect the private sector. They have provided encouragement and support. They have been open to consideration of our recommendations. They have included us in the development of key documents such as the recent National Infrastructure Protection Plan (NIPP). Recognizing the importance of cyber securityand communications, Undersecretary Foresman has recently directed his Deputy Under Secretary, Robert Zitz, to provide day-to-day oversight of the NCSD and the National Communications System, which together constitute the new Cyber Security and Telecommunications organization. Our leadership has met with Mr. Zitz and we are impressed with how quickly he has picked up the reins and the approaches he is espousing. In short, they are trying as hard as anyone can—within current government restrictions on private sector relationships—to develop, nurture and grow a valuable and essential partnership for critical infrastructure protection.

There are many challenges remaining for us to address and new ones are sure to arise. We look forward to meeting those challenges with them and with their successors.

IT–ISAC and the ISAC Council

PDD 63 called for industry establishment of Information Sharing and Analysis Centers (ISACs). The Information Technology (IT) sector coordinator, Mr. Harris Miller, President of the Information Technology Association of America (ITAA) and other sector leaders began developing the necessary charter documents and reaching out to potential members. On January 16, 2001, in a press conference held at the Department of Commerce, 19 founding members formally announced the IT–ISAC. The mission of the IT–ISAC is to provide

- Trusted and confidential reporting, exchange and analysis of sensitive cyber and physical information concerning incidents, threats, attacks, vulnerabilities, solutions, countermeasures, and best security practices.
- A trusted mechanism enabling the systematic and confidential exchange of member information with strong and enforceable legal protections.
- Leadership visibility for IT–ISAC members with public and private enterprises on cyber security processes and information sharing issues.

A sampling of the value of IT–ISAC membership includes:
- Access to Sensitive Threat, Vulnerability and Analytical Products
- Collaboration in a Trusted Forum—vetted, trusted and confidential
- Anonymity for Members—within industry and to government
- Access to Cross Sector and Government Information, Contacts and Tools
- Emergency Response Coordination, Operational Practices, and Exercises

In July 2001, the IT–ISAC went operational through a 24/7 operations center manned by their contract with Internet Security Systems. July 2001 also found them helping coordinate the response to a new form of malicious software, Code Red. On September 11, 2001, they helped to support the response activities and a few days later helped to coordinate the response to another cyber threat, NIMDA.

In 2002, the IT–ISAC established formal information sharing memoranda of understanding (MOUs) with the Financial Services, Electricity and Communications ISACs. In 2003, it helped to establish the ISAC Council, an informal, voluntary, cross-sector body, consisting of the leadership of the active sector ISACs. Mr. John Sabo, the current IT–ISAC President, is also the current Chairman of the ISAC Council. 2003 also saw the IT–ISAC start daily cross-sector cyber security collaboration calls for all ISACs and government agencies (including DHS) which adhere to the MOU information sharing agreements.

Since then the IT–ISAC has continued to mature and expand its capabilities. In 2005, they hired a full time Executive Director, Mr. Scott Algeier. In addition to the daily cyber calls, they host twice weekly cyber technical calls which can dive deeply into technical issues and analysis, for example, those associated with emerging exploits or newly released patches. And they have recently added a weekly physical issues call which supports cross-sector sharing of information regarding physical incidents, vulnerabilities and related matters.

Throughout 2005, IT–ISAC leadership was at the forefront of efforts to form an IT Sector Coordinating Council (IT SCC). SCC's were requested of the critical infrastructures by DHS and Homeland Security Presidential Directive 7 (HSPD 7) and further detailed in the National Partnership Model of the President's National Infrastructure Advisory Council (NIAC). SCCs are intended to be broadly representative of their sector and to work with DHS, Sector Specific Agencies (SSAs) and other organizations in developing strategies and policies for critical infrastructure protection. In January 2006, the IT SCC was formalized and in May it recognized the IT–ISAC as the sector's official operational information sharing mechanism.

> "For operations, analysis and information sharing, the Information Technology Information Sharing and Analysis Center (IT–ISAC) is recognized and endorsed by the Information Technology Sector Coordinating Council (IT SCC) as our lead for the IT sector. The IT–ISAC has served since 2001 and will continue to serve as the main vehicle for communicating information about threats, vulnerabilities and incidents, especially through its Operations Center on a 24/7/365 basis. It is also our main vehicle for information analysis."
>
> IT SCC Chair and Vice Chair Letter to Asst. Sec. Robert Stephan dated 5/26/06

Looking to the Future
Assistant Secretary for Cyber Security and Telecommunciations

In his Second Stage Review, Secretary Michael Chertoff proposed the establishment of an Assistant Secretary position for cyber security and telecommunications to "centralize the coordination of the efforts to protect the technological infrastructure."[1]

The IT Sector Coordinating Council, the IT–ISAC, and the other bodies I have briefly described, stand ready to welcome and work with the new Assistant Secretary from the moment he or she is announced. We have no doubts that it is in the interests of all of us to partner with him or her to address our common security concerns which cannot be addressed by each of us alone.

Even before announcement by DHS of this Assistant Secretary position, the IT Sector leadership had long advocated a senior Cyber Security executive (IT and

---

[1] "Statement of Secretary Michael Chertoff, U.S. Department of Homeland Security, Before the United States Senate Committee on Commerce, Science, and Transportation." July 19, 2005.

Communications) for long term leadership, visibility, making the case for resources, and giving the issue area stature commensurate with the growing risks as IT and Communications become ever more critical to so many of our most important societal functions. The ideal appointee to this new position

- must be credible to both government and industry,
- must be open to new ideas and recognize the value of experienced input,
- must be a strong leader who can build and maintain trusted partnerships, and
- must convey and get support for a vision of success and a path to achieve it.

In addition, he or she will need the commitment of DHS and Administration leadership to succeed. That commitment must strive to ensure the new Assistant Secretary is

- empowered and supported with the resources to succeed,
- supported by positive, "can-do" legal advisers willing to break new ground for the close, trusted relationships required for critical infrastructure protection,
- unhampered to readily and effectively partner and communicate with the private sector, including
  - unhampered by administrative and bureaucratic trivia,
  - unhampered by excessive diversion from priorities, and
  - unhampered by well meaning but inappropriately applied restrictions.

Prioritize and Focus

The new Assistant Secretary must avoid and be protected from chasing the issue of the day or week. To avoid that trap, he or she must ensure that lower priorities are handled as and where needed in the organization but focus his or her attention and that of senior management and oversight on the main priorities

Congress can help empower the new Assistant Secretary by helping to set the right priorities, ensuring resources to achieve them, removing inappropriate and hampering restrictions and providing oversight to the priorities while avoiding diversion of time and attention to minor items

Trusted Partnership

Trusted partnership is a key, critical priority. For critical infrastructure protection, the directly involved key personnel from Government and industry must develop into a well trained, close knit team. The current leadership at DHS has made huge strides to improving partnership but still appear to be hampered by perhaps conservative interpretation and application of laws and regulations rightly intended for protection of a procurement or regulatory relationship, not the national security partnership that Homeland Security needs. Our sectors are complex, evolutionary and robust. Regulation and mandates cannot achieve the intelligent preparedness and response capabilities that thoughtful, voluntary partnership and teamwork can achieve. The best partnership and teamwork is fostered through physical co-location and daily interaction in planning, training and executing—just as in any successful sports team or military unit.

Physical Co-Location for Crisis Coordination—Build on the NCC

A top priority for continuing preparedness and timely response must be physical co-location and frequent daily interaction of representatives of all key players—industry and government—for crisis response management. Ultimately, we execute well that which we develop thoughtfully and practice carefully, learning and improving as we go. Writing a plan for winning isn't enough. I suggest that DHS build on the 20+ years experience with the NCC. Continue to strengthen NCC interoperation with other key 24/7 operations such as those operated by ISACs. Add representatives from other, time-critical ("millisecond sectors"). Add others in time, with core group representation (i.e., representation from the most important organizations for response in the sector or entity.)

National Crisis Coordination Center

The concept of a jointly (industry and government) manned, National Crisis Coordination Center has been around for at least a few years now. In 2004, the Early Warning Task Force begun as one of the National Cyber Security Summit task forces, recommended [2] creation of a national crisis Coordination Center to:

- House government, industry and academic security experts, both physical and cyber, to bridge the cultural barriers that have hampered a true partnership in counterterrorism and cyber security

---

[2] National Early Warning Task Force Recommendation, A NATIONAL CRISIS COORDINATION CENTER, National Cyber Security Partnership, March 2004

- Jointly prepare, exercise, evaluate and update National Joint Crisis Response plans to prevent, detect and respond
- Operate joint watch centers
- Conduct joint exercises at the national level to train and test the plans
- Conduct joint field training at the regional level to train and further test the plans
- Respond jointly to traditional natural events, as well as malicious events
- Proactively share intelligence—both national security and law enforcement
- Include a secure, compartmented intelligence facility staffed equally with government and private sector representatives, as well as appropriate state, local and other representation
- Proactively address priority remediation of systemic vulnerabilities in national level infrastructures

In March 2006, the NSTAC's Next Generation Networks Report recommended a Joint Coordination Center.[3]

A joint coordination center for industry and Government should be established. This would be a cross-sector industry/Government facility with a round-the-clock watch, and would be brought up to full strength during emergencies. Such a center would improve communications between industry and Government as well as among industry members, and would incorporate and be modeled on the NCC.

The center should be a Government-funded, appropriately equipped facility, manned jointly by experts from all key sectors. In a fully converged NGN environment, everything will be interconnected and interdependent to a greater degree, and thus means of coordinating among all key sectors must exist. Physically collocated, joint manning is vital to achieve the high level of interpersonal trust needed for sharing sensitive specific information and to achieve the level of mutual credibility required in a fast-paced decision-oriented environment. It should provide the full set of planning, collaboration, and decision-making tools for those experts to work, whether together as a whole or in focused subgroups. Industry is at times hesitant to share information with the Government because it is unsure of how the information will be used, and Government-to-industry information sharing should also be improved.[4] DHS has a vision for how HSOC will function to improve information sharing; however, the HSOC's current operational interface to the private sector [the National Infrastructure Coordination Center (NICC)] is nascent and needs further development. An environment of trust must be established. A joint operations center could play a key role in fostering that environment and in enhancing HSOC operations. In addition, appropriately cleared industry experts collocated in a joint coordination center with their Government counterparts could assist the Homeland Infrastructure Threat and Risk Analysis Center (HITRAC), the DHS intelligence analysis arm, in performing its analytical and reporting functions, helping to ensure that HITRAC products are more complete, credible and useful.

The Inspector General at DHS has also stated, "If the partnership between the federal government and private sector is to be successful, another key requirement is establishing a permanent physical location or forum so that critical and non-critical sectors can interface with one another and their federal counterparts. This is essential to developing and maintaining long-term collaborative relationships."[5]

NCC Relocation—an Immediate Concern

Since its establishment, the National Coordinating Center for Telecommunications (NCC) has been housed in the Defense Information Systems Agency (DISA) headquarters facility. That location was natural because the same facility housed the National Communication System (NCS) which served as the support Secretariat for the NSTAC and also was assigned responsibility for the jointly manned NCC. That location turned out to be invaluable for trusted, sensitive information sharing. It also housed or came to house DISA's Global Network Operations and Security Center (GNOSC) and its subordinate Defense Department computer emergency response team (CERT), and the Department of Defense Joint Task Force—Global Network Operations (JTF–GNO). The synergy and trusted interaction between and among these entities has become important to all participants for both national security and emergency response purposes. Unfortunately, current plans call for relocating the NCC to co-locate it with the US–CERT operated by DHS.

---

[3] Next Generation Networks Task Force Report, NSTAC, March 28, 2006.

[4] Both these observations were confirmed at the August 2005 NGN Incident Response Subject Matter Experts meetings. See Appendix D of the Next Generation Networks Task Force Report, NSTAC, March 28, 2006.

[5] A Review of the Top Officials 3 Exercise, DHS OIG Report OIG–06–07, p. 24 (Nov. 2005).

We should strongly consider the wisdom of separating the NCC from the DoD entities with which it is located. Instead we should encourage the leadership of the DoD, DISA and DHS to consider an approach that could strengthen the value for all: co-locate the US–CERT and other NCSD operational response elements with the NCC *and* their counterpart DoD elements. While each has a different mission and set of customers, they are all ultimately looking at overlapping sets of data and similar problem sets. Co-location will allow for greater interaction and synergy, leading to enhanced efficiency and value for all their "customers."

Because the Base Realignment and Closure process is expected to relocate DISA in a few years, part of the examination of the value for the nation in achieving multi-organization co-location will have to be an examination of facility alternatives. But that should not deter us from at least exploring the potential benefits that could be achieved for the nation and both our national and homeland security. Ultimately, the co-location facility could be part of the National Crisis Coordination Center which I have already described.

My industry colleagues and I would be happy to participate in such an examination.

Congress Can Help
Support Examination of NCC Co-location and Expansion to a National Crisis Coordination Center

Look at co-location of the NCC, the US-CERT, the JTF–GNO and other existing similar entities for advantages to their missions, their "customers" and the nation. Similarly, examine the National Crisis Coordination Center (NCCC) concept in detail and strongly support its implementation if it holds up to your scrutiny as many of us expect it will. Be sure to include international liaison in the NCCC. Many of our allies are even more closely intertwined with us in the Cyber world than in the physical world. But in both, the interdependencies can be enormous. In particular, with Canada, many of our key critical infrastructures and dependencies are mutually shared across our common border.

Focus on Priorities

Use your oversight and appropriations powers to work with DHS and the private sector in the establishment of Cyber Security priorities. Then follow-up to ensure DHS has the necessary resources to implement those priorities.

Create a Better Environment

Congress can create a better environment for homeland security partnership, helping us achieve a tight knit, superbly prepared, professional team with high morale, and a commitment to each other to succeed. The current environment for government and industry interaction is designed rightly to prevent fraud and abuse in procurement or regulatory matters or other areas where an unscrupulous actor might try to further a personal or organizational agenda, contrary to the public good. In many ways, those rules implicitly require Government personnel to maintain an "arms length," almost adversary relationship. At the very least, it implicitly impugns motives before the fact. But Homeland Security partnerships must be close, trusted, and non-public. Could the Washington Redskins or any professional team succeed if their members were not allowed to get together to plan and train out of sight of their opponents when needed?

We cannot do away with protection against fraud and abuse. But the close teamwork and rapid response requirements of Homeland Security and Critical Infrastructure Protection demand high levels of interpersonal trust that can only be developed through frequent interaction, including informal, relationship building interaction. To accomplish this and still protect against fraud and abuse, I believe that we will need to replace the rigid rules and bureaucratically slow exception handling processes with alternative systems that provide strong, independent oversight to detect, report, halt and punish fraud and abuse but encourage true partnership, trusted relationships and team building, treating all participants as if they are members of the same organization/team, operating under the same code of ethics but free to form trusted and close relationships.

Examine Innovative Ways to Encourage Private Sector Active Participation

Congress might be able to help encourage even more private sector participation in critical infrastructure protection through private sector bodies such as the SCCs and ISACs. Here are a few examples which might be worth exploring.

Value Proposition

Congress and the DHS should work with SCCs, ISACs and other private sector institutions to develop a compelling value proposition with industry to further im-

88

prove our working relationship for critical infrastructure protection and expand improved cyber security behavior. Not doing so is contrary to our national and homeland security interest. Many companies and other private sector institutions understand this. But many still do not. We need to make the value proposition compelling so that the vast majority—and all the critical ones—understand and pro-actively participate.

Congressional and Executive Support for SCCs and ISACs

Carefully examine the positive role that DHS and Administration executive leadership could and should play in encouraging sector members to participate in their respective SCCs and ISACs. Private sector leaders responded to previous Government requests and have expended significant resources to create the partnership model organizations requested. But when it comes to encouraging sector members to join those bodies and actively participate in them, Government executives have been strangely absent or quiet for the most part. Also, in some cases they have reached out through other organizations not formed for these specific purposes. The net effect of their silence or misaimed outreach is contrary to the very goals they envisioned achieving when they asked the private sector to form ISACs and SCCs.

Simply put, they should always turn first to the organizations they asked us to form to fit their model for working with them. And they should not be shy about encouraging sector members to join those organizations (ISACs and SCCs), even to the extent of expressing unhappiness with important sector "core" players who fail to do so. If there are any rules in place that impede such demonstrable support, they should be revisited swiftly and decisively.

Technical and Operational Support

The ultimate goal of our partnership model is to create an infrastructure environment that is intended to deter attacks as much as feasible and operationally prepared to respond, recover and reconstitute to any attack or emergency as rapidly and effectively as feasible. Operational preparedness and success will depend ultimately on a partnership that is focused on operations even more than on policy. The recommendations I have made for a jointly manned, National Crisis Coordination Center (NCCC) will help significantly to shift to an operational focus. But it will also take working out and testing our individual and collective Concepts of Operations (CONOPS), constantly improving them so our operational metrics continually improve. The best solutions may call for cross sector or even government to industry provisioning of technical and operational support. For example, DHS support to operational ISACs might be appropriate. Operational readiness and improvement should be one of our highest priorities.

Congressional Charters

Examine the Potential Value of a Congressional Charter for established SCCs and ISACs. If a National Crisis Coordination Center is supported, consider a Congressional Charter for it as well. Congressional Charters would give Congress enhanced visibility into their functioning and would allow for periodic GAO audit. They would also help many SCCs and ISACs recruit the broad membership and participation they need from their sectors.

Procurement

Consider using procurement in DHS, or even government-wide, as a carrot for greater private sector participation and proactive, operational commitments.

Congressional Awareness and Education

Finally, to help prepare you for the increasingly complex issues of the Cyber Security Age, I suggest you consider forming a bipartisan House caucus for cyber security (IT and communications) to provide a forum for educating staff and members on the relevant issues.

ATTACHMENT

SUMMARY OF A FEW KEY CYBER SECURITY AND TELECOMMUNICATIONS PARTNERSHIPS AND KEY INITIATIVES

NSTAC

President Ronald Reagan created the National Security Telecommunications Advisory Committee (NSTAC) by Executive Order 12382 in September 1982. Composed of up to 30 industry chief executives representing many of the major communications and network service providers and information technology, finance, and aerospace companies, the NSTAC provides industry-based advice and expertise to the President on issues and problems related to implementing national security and emergency preparedness (NS/EP) communications policy. Since its inception, the

NSTAC has addressed a wide range of policy and technical issues regarding communications, information systems, information assurance, critical infrastructure protection, and other NS/EP communications concerns.

NS/EP communications enable the Government to make an immediate and coordinated response to all emergencies, whether caused by a natural disaster, such as a hurricane, an act of domestic terrorism, such as the Oklahoma City bombing and the September 11th attacks, a man-made disaster, or a cyber attack. NS/EP communications allow the President and other senior Administration officials to be continually accessible, even under stressed conditions.

The NSTAC has addressed numerous issues in the past 24 years. A few examples illustrate NSTAC's capabilities to address NS/EP communications issues in today's environment: the establishment of the National Coordinating Center for Telecommunications (NCC); the implementation of the Government and NSTAC Network Security Information Exchange (NSIE) process; the Telecommunications Service Priority (TSP) program; Government Emergency Telecommunications Service (GETS) and Wireless Priority Service (WPS); and the examination of the NS/EP implications of Internet technologies and the vulnerabilities of converged networks. These accomplishments are briefly described below.

NCC—From "NSTAC Report to the President on the National Coordinating Center," May 10, 2006

The NCC was established to fulfill a critical need for a national coordinating mechanism to organize and manage the initiation and restoration of NS/EP communications services. This need was identified at the dawn of the divestiture of AT&T and the height of the Cold War. As Government increasingly relied on commercial communications services and no longer had a single point of contact (POC) for the industry, Government needed a joint industry and Government-staffed organization to coordinate emergency requests. The NCC became operational on January 3, 1984.

The National Coordinating Center (NCC) has been the hub for coordinating the initiation and restoration of national security and emergency preparedness (NS/EP) communications services for more than 20 years—supporting four administrations and evolving as threats and national priorities have shifted. Following the September 11, 2001, terrorist attacks, the NCC proved its value to the Nation as it supported the restoration of communications in the New York and Washington, D.C., areas. The NCC has also repeatedly shown its strength during hurricane recovery efforts, including Hurricane Katrina.

. . .the NSTAC recommended designating the NCC as the Information Sharing and Analysis Center (ISAC) for telecommunications in 1999.

With the establishment of the Department of the Homeland Security (DHS) and the transfer of the National Communications System (NCS) to the new department in 2003, the NCC also has made the transition to DHS.

The primary mission of the NCC throughout its history has been to coordinate the restoration and provisioning of communications services for NS/EP users during natural disasters, armed conflicts, and terrorist attacks. Significant events such as the Hinsdale, Illinois, central office fire, the Oklahoma terrorist bombing, the events of September 11, 2001, and Hurricane Katrina have proved the value of this partnership. During a crisis, Government personnel communicate NS/EP requirement priorities to industry, and industry representatives assist the Government in developing situational awareness by providing restoration status information. Having the representatives in one location ensures a smoother restoration effort. The NCC's all-hazards response depends on the flexible application of NCS resources, such as its priority service programs (e.g., Government Emergency Telecommunications Service, Wireless Priority Service, and Telecommunications Service Priority [TSP] Program).

During day-to-day operations, NCC members work on plans and share information on vulnerabilities and threats to the telecom infrastructure. Planning activities include developing lessons learned following events, creating comprehensive service restoration plans, planning for continuity of operations (COOP)/continuity of Government (COG) activities, and participating in exercise planning. In addition, the NCC works with international emergency response partners, including the North Atlantic Treaty Organization (NATO), International Telecommunication Union (ITU), and Canada, on crisis communications and mutual assistance.

In 2000, the NCC was designated the ISAC for telecommunications per the guidance in the 1998 Presidential Decision Directive 63 (PDD-63), Protecting America's Critical Infrastructures, which encouraged the private sector to establish ISACs to "serve as the mechanism for gathering, analyzing, appropriately sanitizing and disseminating private sector information." As part of the ISAC mission, the NCC collects and shares information about threats, vulnerabilities, intrusions, and anomalies from the communications industry, Government, and other sources. Analysis on in-

*formation is performed with the goal of averting or mitigating impact on the commu-
nications infrastructure.*

*The NCC has historically been an operational element and as such does not fall
under provisions of the Federal Advisory Committee Act (FACA). A June 1, 1983, letter to the NCS from Assistant Attorney General William F. Baxter discussed issues
of incident management and information sharing for the proposed National Coordinating Mechanism (NCM) (which became the NCC) and noted that such an organization posed no significant antitrust problems.*

*. . .Since the transition to DHS, the NCC has been involved in additional critical
infrastructure protection (CIP) activities. As part of the implementation of Homeland
Security Presidential Directive (HSPD) 7, DHS is tasked with identifying,
prioritizing, and protecting the Nation's critical infrastructure. Through the NCC,
the NCS often coordinates data calls on the identification of assets, coordinates planning for national special security events (NSSE), and provides impact analyses. In
the future, NCC industry members may be asked to further assist in the risk assessment process as detailed in the sector's Sector-Specific Plan.*

NSIE—From "GUIDE TO UNDERSTANDING THE NATIONAL COORDINATING
CENTER FOR TELECOMMUNICATIONS AND THE NETWORK SECURITY IN-
FORMATION EXCHANGES," PREPARED BY THE OFFICE OF THE MANAGER,
NATIONAL COMMUNICATIONS SYSTEM, MARCH 2001

*In April 1990, the Chairman of the National Security Council's (NSC) Policy Co-
ordinating Committee—National Security Telecommunications and Information
Systems requested the Manager, NCS, identify what action should be taken by
Government and industry to protect critical national security telecommunications
from the "hacker" threat. . . .In response to the NSC tasking, the Manager, NCS
and the NSTAC established separate, but closely coordinated, NSIEs. In May
1991, the NSIE charters were finalized, and Government departments and agencies and NSTAC companies designated their NSIE representatives, chairmen,
and vice-chairmen. The first joint meeting of the Government and NSTAC
NSIEs was held in June 1991.*

*The Government and NSTAC NSIEs meet jointly approximately every two months.
The NSIEs provide a working forum to identify issues involving penetration or ma-
nipulation of software and databases affecting NS/EP telecommunications. The
NSIEs share information with the objectives of:*

  • *Learning more about intrusions into and vulnerabilities affecting the
    PN—Developing recommendations for reducing network security
    vulnerabilities*
  • *Assessing network risks affecting network assurance*
  • *Acquiring threat and threat mitigation information*
  • *Providing expertise to the NSTAC on which to base network security rec-
    ommendations to the President.*

**The success of the NSIEs is based in large part on the establishment of
trusted interpersonal relationships. Participants—government and industry—must hold requisite security clearances and sign individual non-disclosure agreements. The organizations sending participants to the NSIEs must
also sign organizational non-disclosure agreements.**

TSP—From NCS Web site

*Telecommunications Service Priority (TSP) provides service vendors with a Fed-
eral Communications Commission (FCC) mandate for prioritizing service requests by identifying those services critical to NS/EP. A telecommunications
service with a TSP assignment is assured of receiving full attention by the service vendor before a non-TSP service.*

From briefing "NCS Roles During the Attack on America," Deputy Manager,
NCS, August 9, 2002
Nearly 40,000 TSP circuits enrolled by NCS prior to 9/11 tragedy
  TSP vital in accelerating the opening of Wall Street on 9/17
    *Major coordination in restoration of telecommunications for Broad
    Street switches—major role to restore stock and bond markets*
  NCS supported nearly 600 provisioning requests following 11 Sep 01
    46 organizations (incl. FBI, FEMA , FRB, Port Authority, DoD)

GETS—From NCS Web site

*Implemented in the early 1990's, Government Emergency Telecommunications
Service (GETS) is an emergency phone service provided by the National Communications System (NCS) in the Information Analysis and Infrastructure Protection Division of the Department of Homeland Security. GETS supports federal,
state, local, tribal, industry, and non-governmental organization (NGO) per-*

*sonnel in performing their National Security and Emergency Preparedness (NS/
EP) missions. GETS provides emergency access and priority processing in the
local and long distance segments of the Public Switched Telephone Network
(PSTN). It is intended to be used in an emergency or crisis situation when the
PSTN is congested and the probability of completing a call over normal or other
alternate telecommunication means has significantly decreased.*

From briefing "NCS Roles During the Attack on America," Deputy Manager,
NCS, August 9, 2002

*The AT&T long distance network carried a record 431 million call attempts on
Sept. 11, 101 million more than the previous high-traffic day.*
Massive congestion in WTC & Pentagon areas
    Over 10,000 GETS calls in WTC/Pentagon areas
        Over 95% completion rate—Highest calling in first 48 hours
    GETS PIN Cards:
        Over 1,500 key personnel made GETS calls
        Over 20,000 GETS PIN cards issued following events of September 11th

WPS—From NCS Web site

*Wireless Priority Service (WPS), is the wireless complement to GETS. In the
early 1990's, the OMNCS initiated efforts based on NSTAC recommendations, to
develop and implement a nationwide cellular priority access capability in support of national security and emergency preparedness (NS/EP) telecommunications and pursued a number of activities to improve cellular call completion
during times of network congestion. Subsequently, as a result of a petition filed
by the NCS in October 1995, the FCC released a Second Report and Order
[FCC–00–242, July 13, 2000] (R&O) on wireless Priority Access Service (PAS).
The R&O offers Federal liability relief for NS/EP wireless carriers if the service
is implemented in accordance with uniform operating procedures. The FCC
made PAS voluntary, found it to be in the public interest, and defined five priority levels for NS/EP wireless calls.*

*Wireless network congestion was widespread on September 11, 2001. With wire-
less traffic demand estimated at up to 10 times normal in the affected areas and
double nationwide, the need for wireless priority service became a critical and
urgent National requirement. In response, the National Security Council requested that the NCS deploy a nationwide priority access queuing system for
wireless networks.*

*From briefing "NCS Roles During the Attack on America," Deputy Manager,
NCS, August 9, 2002:*
    *Verizon Wireless experienced a 50 to 100 percent increase nationwide. Wire-
less networks remained near saturation in NY through September 28th.*
    *Cingular Wireless' attempted calls ballooned by 400 percent in Washington
and 1000 percent in its N.J. Switching Center*

PDD 63 and Sector Coordinators

Presidential Decision Directive 63 (PDD 63) was released in May 1998. It ordered
the development of sector-specific critical infrastructure protection plans and established the role of private industry sector coordinators. The Information & Communications Sector as then designated under PDD 63, had four organizations sharing
the sector coordinator role: the Cellular Telecommunications and Internet Association (CTIA), the Information Technology Association of America (ITAA); the Telecommunications Industry Association (TIA); and the United States Telecom Association (USTA).

Important early contributions of the Sector coordinators included
- developing internal sector awareness
- organizing voluntary sector participation in planning
- leading the way in the formation of Information Sharing and Analysis
  Centers for Information Technology and Telecommunications
- developing the I&C Sector National Strategy Input for Critical
Infrastructure and Cyberspace Security, May 2002

PCIS

The Partnership for Critical Infrastructure Security (PCIS) consists generally of
the leadership (usually the Chairs) of the organized Sector Coordinating Councils
for the various critical infrastructures. The PCIS coordinates cross sector critical infrastructure protection interests and initiatives within the private sector and with
the Government under the partnership model described within the National Infrastructure Protection Plan

NCSP (Santa Clara Dec 03 Summit, TFs, reports, Wye I, Wye II)

The National Cyber Security Partnership (NCSP) combines representatives from government, industry and academia working together to harden the nation's cyber defenses. The partnership provides a forum, structure and common agenda for interdisciplinary, cross-industry information exchange with government. Lead organizations of the partnership are: the Business Software Alliance, Information Technology Association of America, TechNet and the U.S. Chamber of Commerce. The public-private partnership was formed during the National Cyber Security Summit on December 3, 2003, in Santa Clara, California, which aimed to gather cyber security experts across disciplines to embark on a work program to develop recommendations for implementing key challenges posed in the 2003 National Strategy to Secure Cyberspace. The partnership established five task forces comprised of cyber security experts from industry, academia and government. Each task force was led by two or more co-chairs. The NCSP-sponsoring trade associations act as secretariats in managing task force work flow and logistics. The task forces included:

Awareness for Home Users and Small Businesses

Cyber Security Early Warning

Corporate Governance

Security Across the Software Development Life Cycle

Technical Standards and Common Criteria

The resulting task force recommendations in 2004 were provided to DHS. Many are still valid an valuable.

In follow-up to the National Cyber Security Summit and the reports of the task forces, DHS' National Cyber Security Division hosted a government and private sector exchange at the Wye River Conference Center in Maryland in January 2005. A second follow-up exchange ("Wye II") was hosted by the NCSP in Annapolis, MD, in September 2005. Many of the original Summit Task Forces' Recommendations continue to be brought up as potentially valuable.

CIPAC—extracted from DHS sources

In March 2006, the Department of Homeland Security established the Critical Infrastructure Partnership Advisory Council (CIPAC) to facilitate effective coordination between Federal infrastructure protection programs with the infrastructure protection activities of the private sector and of state, local, territorial and tribal governments.

The CIPAC represents a partnership between government and critical infrastructure/key resource (CI/KR) owners and operators and provides a forum in which they can engage in a broad spectrum of activities to support and coordinate critical infrastructure protection.

CIPAC membership will encompass CI/KR owner/operator institutions and their designated trade or equivalent organizations that are identified as members of existing Sector Coordinating Councils (SCCs). It is also includes representatives from Federal, state, local and tribal governmental entities identified as members of existing Government Coordinating Councils (GCCs) for each sector

IDWG—extracted from DHS sources

The Internet Disruption Working Group (IDWG) is a DHS hosted, informal gathering of industry and government Internet technical operation experts who collaboratively explore vulnerability issues and identify recommended actions to address them. The IDWG is beginning to establish important, trusted interpersonal relationships amongst government and industry technical experts. The IDWG was established by NCSD in partnership with the National Communications System (NCS), in response to security concerns surrounding the growing dependency of critical infrastructures and national security and emergency preparedness users on the Internet for communications, operational functions, and essential services.

The IDWG's near-term objectives are to improve the resiliency and recovery of Internet functions in the event of a cyber-related incident of national significance; work with both government and private sector stakeholders to identify and prioritize protective measures necessary to prevent and respond to major Internet disruptions; and assess the operational dependencies of critical infrastructure sectors on the Internet. The 2005 IDWG Forum identified specific areas for action by both government and private sector stakeholders, including risk assessments, information sharing, protective measures, research and development, and Internet development issues. The IDWG is engaging with both public and private stakeholders to address these action items. The IDWG also plans to hold future forums and tabletop exercises, including an IDWG Tabletop Exercise, on June 15, 2006, to maintain both a pulse of the issues and an understanding of existing capabilities.

Mr. LUNGREN. Thank you very much for your testimony.

Now, we would hear from Mr. David Barron, the chairman of the Telecommunications Sector Coordination Council.

STATEMENT OF DAVID M. BARRON, CHAIR, TELECOMMUNICATIONS SECTOR COORDINATING COUNCIL

Mr. BARRON. Good afternoon, Mr. Chairman and fellow members of the subcommittee. It is an honor and a pleasure to be here with you today and I thank you for the opportunity to discuss this very important topic, the future of cybersecurity and telecommunications.

I am David Barron. I am assistant vice president for federal relations and national security for Bell South, here in our Washington Office, but I am appearing today as the chair of the Communications Sector Coordinating Council. My testimony reflects my personal views as the chair of the council and not the views of Bell South.

Sector-specific planning and coordination are addressed to private sector and government coordinating councils that are established for each sector through the national infrastructure protection plan.

Sector coordinating councils are comprised of private sector entities, representatives. Government coordinating councils are comprised of representatives from government agencies, state, local and tribal entities.

Established in 2005, the Communications Sector Coordinating Council has over 25 owners and operators and associations represented on the council today and we anticipate adding new members, as we continue to broaden our membership.

While Homeland Security Presidential Directive 7 defined our sector as telecommunications, we in the industry feel that communications is a more representative title and that represents our diverse membership more accurately.

Our membership today includes wire line, wireless, satellite, equipment manufacturers and Internet service providers, among others. We are also actively trying to expand the membership to include cable telephony, emergency service providers, and broadcasters, so that the Communications Sector Coordinating Council truly represents the breadth of this dynamic sectors.

One of the sectors we call, as Guy said, the millisecond sector because of the nature of how our sector works.

The Communications Sector Coordinating Council is currently engaged in a wide variety of activities not only with our government colleagues, but also with the Department of Homeland Security, as well as other sector coordinating councils on a number of initiatives the foremost of which, and you have heard about it today, is the creation of the sector-specific plan.

We are well into that and we are anxious to get that project finished as soon as possible.

In addition to the sector-specific plan, the Communications Sector Coordinating Council is engaged in several other important activities and I think the point is, as Guy said, we are not on hold. We are working every day to ensure the best security we can for the nation.

These other activities include pandemic flu planning, national coordinating center, regional coordination concepts, post–Katrina issues, such as access, credentialing and emergency responder status as it relates to the Stafford Act, emergency wireless protocols, and many other activities.

Finally, the world of communications often has considerable interaction and interdependencies with information technology, another critical infrastructure identified through HSPD–7. As such, the Communications Sector Coordinating Council has established a close working relationship with the Information Technology Sector Coordinating Council on issues of mutual concern.

In September, the Communications and Information Technology Councils will be holding the first ever joint meeting with all four councils present, both communications, IT and the government counterparts, to discuss cross-sector issues, such as the creation of sector-specific plans that are complementary and support of each other.

With the support of Under Secretary Foresman, the assistant secretary for infrastructure protection, Bob Steffen, has overseen many of these initiatives while in the acting assistant secretary for cybersecurity and telecommunications position and while serving as the manager of the national communications systems, known as the NCS.

We are pleased with the progress that has been made, but the industry would welcome additional focus brought to bear by a dedicated assistant secretary for cybersecurity and telecommunications.

Obviously, we should view all critical infrastructures and key resources defined in HSPD–7 as critically important to the nation. However, communications and information technology are unique in that they underlie and support all the other sectors.

Each of the other sectors depends upon computer systems, voice networks, broadband systems, wireless networks, and countless other structures and services provided by the communications and IT communities. Those sectors are equally critical in support of the nation's homeland security mission.

While DHS has been very helpful and responsive in many of these matters, there are areas in which the private sector would specifically like to see continued progress and improvement.

First, while the current team of leadership at DHS has done a good job working with the sector, the position of assistant secretary for cybersecurity and telecommunications remains vacant. As I stated earlier in my testimony, Assistant Secretary Steffen has done an admirable job in working with the communications and IT sectors, but a dedicated assistant secretary could dramatically strengthen this critical public-private partnership.

Second, a clear definition of the mission needs to be established. What does cybersecurity and telecommunications really mean as it relates to national security, homeland security and emergency preparedness? In other words, what is the problem we are trying to solve?

There is such a wide range of threats and vulnerabilities that a clear vision of the problem tied to priorities is essential.

Third, DHS needs to clearly define roles and responsibilities for all of those involved in this process, and this comes back to the understanding of the problem and a clear strategy based on risk assessment and priorities. By clarifying who is in charge of what, more will be accomplished in an efficient and effective manner.

Finally, and I think very importantly, DHS should recognize that the private sector is willing and fully committed to this partnership. If this framework is truly intended to be a partnership, then more emphasis needs to be placed on ensuring there is a trusted relationship between the public and private sectors, which is in the best interest of the nation's security.

For example, the national coordinating center for communications, the NCC, is a model to follow for the partnership that is mandated by the future. In the NCC, government and industry sit together every day to prepare for and to respond to events that threaten the nation's communications networks.

The NCC has had a long history of success. I think this model could and should be expanded to include other infrastructure, like information technology and electric power.

As I close, I would like to, again, thank the subcommittee for the opportunity to speak today and for your support on these efforts. The partnership framework is incredibly valuable and continues to serve as a conduit for unprecedented cooperation and collaboration between government and private industry.

There is room for improvement, to be sure, but the suggestions I have presented here today are intended to further strengthen those valued interactions and ensure we jointly consider to take steps to secure our homeland.

Thank you, sir.

[The statement of Mr. Barron follows:]

PREPARED STATEMENT OF DAVID M. BARRON

Good Afternoon Mr. Chairman and fellow members of the committee. It is an honor to appear before you today and I thank you for the opportunity to discuss this very important topic, the future of cyber security and telecommunications.

I am David Barron, Assistant Vice President for Federal Relations/National Security with BellSouth Corporation here in our Washington office, but I am appearing today as the Chair of the Communications Sector Coordinating Council (CSCC). My testimony reflects my personal views as Chairman of the CSCC and not the views of Bell South.

Let me begin by giving you a brief background on the Sector Partnership Model and the Communications SCC in particular. Homeland Security Presidential Directive 7 (HSPD–7) established the basis for a national coordinated approach to critical infrastructure protection, including the development of the National Infrastructure Protection Plan (NIPP) as well as the Sector Partnership Model. The NIPP defines the organizational structure that provides the framework for coordination of Critical Infrastructure and Key Resources (CI/KR) protection efforts at all levels of government, as well as within and across sectors.

Sector-specific planning and coordination are addressed through private sector and government coordinating councils that are established for each sector. Sector Coordinating Councils (SCCs) are comprised of private sector representatives. Government Coordinating Councils (GCCs) are comprised of representatives of the Sector-Specific Agencies, other Federal departments and agencies, and state, local, and tribal governments.

Established in 2005, the Communications Sector Coordinating Council has over 25 owner/operators and associations represented on the Council and we anticipate adding new members as we continue to broaden our membership. While HSPD–7 defined our sector as "Telecommunications", we in the industry feel that "Communications" is a more encompassing title that represents our diverse membership. Our membership today includes wireline, wireless, satellite, equipment manufacturers, and internet service providers among others. We are also actively trying to expand the membership to include cable telephony, emergency service providers and broadcasters so that our Communications Sector Coordinating Council truly represents the breadth of this dynamic sector; one of the sectors we call the "millisecond" sector due to the nature of how our sector works.

The CSCC is currently engaged in a wide variety of activities not only with our Communications Government Coordinating Council counterparts, but also with the Department of Homeland Security as well as other Sector Coordinating Councils on a number of initiatives, foremost of which is the creation of our Sector Specific Plan.

The NIPP base plan is supported by several Sector Specific Plans (SSPs) that provide further detail on how the critical infrastructure and key resources protection mission of each sector will be carried out. In late August the Communications SCC and GCC held a joint meeting in Washington, D.C. to coordinate on several issues, the most prominent of which is the development of the Sector-Specific Plan (SSP) as I mentioned before. The CSCC and GCC have been actively collaborating on a draft of the Communications SSP, with both Councils providing input and comments throughout the process. This effort is continuing and we are on track to submit the Communications SSP by the end of the year to DHS.

In addition to the SSP, the Communications SCC is engaged in several other important activities, including Pandemic Flu planning, National Coordinating Center (NCC) regional coordination, post-Katrina issues such as access, credentialing, and emergency responder status related to the Stafford Act, emergency wireless protocols, and many other activities.

Finally, the world of Communications often has considerable interaction and interdependencies with Information Technology (another critical infrastructure established by HSPD–7). As such, the Communications SCC has established a close relationship with the Information Technology SCC to work on issues of mutual concern. In September the Communications and Information Technology SCCs and GCCs will be holding the first ever Joint meeting, with all four councils present, to discuss cross-sector issues such as the creation of Sector Specific Plans that are complimentary and supportive of each other.

With the support of Under Secretary Foresman, Assistant Secretary for Infrastructure Protection Bob Stephan has overseen many of these initiatives while in the Acting Assistant Secretary for Cyber Security and Telecommunications position and while serving as the Manager of the National Communications System (NCS). We are pleased with the progress that has been made. But the industry would welcome the additional focus brought to bear by a dedicated Assistant Secretary for Cyber Security and Telecommunications.

Obviously, we should view all the critical infrastructures and key resources defined in HSPD–7 as critically important to the nation. However, Communications and Information Technology is unique in that it underlies and supports all of the other sectors. Each of the other sectors depend upon computer systems, voice networks, broadband systems, wireless networks, and countless other structures and services provided by the Communications and IT communities. As a result, Congress has mandated and DHS has begun implementing strategies and procedures to ensure specific emphasis on these valuable cross-sector interdependencies. For example, the National Infrastructure Protection Plan and the supporting Sector Plans are working very specifically to address this convergence of Communications and Information Technology into what is referred to as the Next Generation Networks. As this work continues, there must be a balanced approach when looking at Cyber Security and Telecommunications. Both sectors are equally critical in support of the Nation's Homeland Security mission.

While DHS has been very helpful and responsive in many of these matters, there are areas in which the private sector would specifically like to see continued progress and improvement. First, while the current team of leadership at DHS, including Under Secretary Foresman, Deputy Under Secretary Robert Zitz, and Assistant Secretary Stephan, have done an excellent job, the position of Assistant Secretary for Cyber Security and Telecommunications remains vacant. As I stated earlier in my testimony, Assistant Secretary Stephan has done an admirable job in working with the Communications and Information Technology community but a dedicated Assistant Secretary could dramatically strengthen this critical public/private partnership.

Second, a clear definition of the mission needs to be established. What does Cyber Security and Telecommunications really mean as it relates to National Security, Homeland Security and Emergency Preparedness? In other words, what is the problem that we are trying to solve? There is such a wide range of threats and vulnerabilities that a clear vision of the problem tied to priorities is essential.

Third, DHS needs to clearly define roles and responsibilities for all of those involved in this process. Again, this comes back to the understanding of the problem and a clear strategy based on risk assessment and priorities. By clarifying who is in charge of what, more will be accomplished in an efficient and effective manner.

Finally, DHS should recognize that the private sector is willing and fully committed to this partnership. If this framework is truly intended to be a partnership, then more emphasis needs to be placed on ensuring there is a trusted relationship between the public and private sectors, which is in the best interest of our Nation's security. For example, the National Coordinating Center for Communications—the NCC—is a model to follow for the partnership that is mandated by the future. In the NCC, government and industry sit together everyday to prepare for and to respond to events that threaten the Nation's communications networks. The NCC has had a long history of success and I think this model could and should be expanded to include other infrastructures like Information Technology/Cyber and Electric Power. The continued health and evolution of the partnership depends not only on private sector participation, but DHS' s recognition of the value of that partnership with a commitment to work more closely with industry.

As I close, I would like to again thank Congress for the opportunity to speak today and for their support in these efforts. The partnership framework is incredibly valuable and continues to serve as a conduit for unprecedented cooperation and collaboration between government and private industry. There is room for improvement to be sure, but the suggestions I have presented here today are intended to further strengthen these valued interactions and ensure we jointly continue to take steps to secure our homeland.

Thank You.

Mr. LUNGREN. Thank you all for your testimony.

We will go to a round of questioning. We promised that we would get you out of here no later than 6:00. So we will see how long that takes us with the members who are here.

Let me begin the questioning by asking you, Mr. Pelgrin, how would you describe the overall priority that the federal government has placed on cyber-related critical infrastructure protection?

Mr. PELGRIN. I believe that they have put a high priority on it. I think that they definitely need to fill the assistant secretary position. But I know that even the undersecretary, that when he was in Virginia, was actually one of our multi-state ISAC members.

So he, from early on, believed very much in cybersecurity. So from my experience, from the governmental experience, from the state and local government, the support that we have received, the direction, the cooperation with the federal government has been excellent.

I think there is always room to improve. I think that there is always a need, both on a state and local government side, to move this forward. I am a big believer that this is to build it as you go and it really is a time to make sure that we have very strict deliverables and get those deliverables executed.

So from a priority perspective, I think that that badly, by not having the assistant secretary position filled, taints all the good work that they are doing and they are doing a lot of good work.

Mr. LUNGREN. Mr. Kurtz, of the six points that you have made, the first, I noted, was lead, lead, lead.

Is that a suggestion that the department is not leading at the present time?

Mr. KURTZ. It would be a suggestion that they are not leading.

Mr. LUNGREN. Are they compromised not leading because of the absence of a leadership position being filled?

Mr. KURTZ. I think so. Certainly, the assistant secretary of cybersecurity and telecommunications will provide some leadership. It is not a panacea, though. I think we have to go higher up the line in the department, as well, to ensure that they are paying attention to the issue at the most senior levels.

I commend Under Secretary Foresman for spending the time today to address this issue up here on the Hill. He was at a committee meeting earlier today, and it is very good to see him here.

Mr. LUNGREN. And I got a deliverable. I got a letter from the secretary answering my questions, from my letter of July 5. Maybe we ought to have these meetings more often.

Mr. KURTZ. If I can, I think it is symptomatic of across the federal government. We have, if you will, a reluctance among senior officials to engage on cyber and I think one of the real reasons it it is not visual. You can't see it, you can't touch it, you can't feel it.

When you go into a cyber?

Mr. LUNGREN. You can't show it to your constituents.

Mr. KURTZ. You can't show it to your constituents, as well. You go into a cyber knock and you look at it and, quite frankly, it can be pretty boring. But this logical system, this nervous system that we depend upon controls every facet of our lives.

And just because we can't see it and taste it and smell it doesn't mean we shouldn't be paying attention to it.

Mr. LUNGREN. Mr. Kurtz, who is further along, in your estimate, the private sector or the federal government, in terms of cybersecurity?

Mr. KURTZ. I think there are elements of the private sector that are quite far along. I would highlight the banking and finance industry. The banking and finance industry has brought incredible sophistication to this space.

Can they do better? Sure. I think the energy, the oil and gas sector is getting more serious about this. I think Doug Bond's program, Doug at least was behind a little bit ago, the logic program that they are doing on working on SCADA control systems and improving the security is a fantastic program and it is a partner program.

So there is work under way in that area. Frankly, I think the other sectors, many of the other sectors have a long way to go.

Mr. LUNGREN. I mean, if we are going to have a team in this, you look at the football analogy, you have got to have both the offense and the defense and the special teams all working together.

I look at this as a partnership opportunity and obligation, private sector-public sector, in part, because 85–90 percent of the critical infrastructure is owned not by the government, but by the private sector.

I would assume that if we have got the cyber world involved in critical infrastructure, that we would have that same sort of percentage. So we have got to be firming up both sides.

And to Mr. Copeland and Mr. Barron, thank you for your testimony and thank you for the work that you are doing. You are doing double-duty, too. I mean, you are doing the work for your companies and you are also doing the work in these coordinating councils.

A general question to the two of you and then maybe if we get time for a second round, I can go into more specifics.

How well is the concept of the coordinating councils working? You are putting a lot of effort into it. Obviously, you think it is worthwhile, because you are both still doing it.

You are getting the cooperation of not only your companies, but like companies. But is government listening? Is government really acting as a partner with you in this coordinating councils?

Do you feel that your time is well spent? And has the experience been such that it is encouraging to have other companies become involved and commit their people to the time that is necessary to actually make a contribution?

Mr. COPELAND. Mr. Chairman, as a general observation, of course, our sector coordinating councils are just getting started. So the answer is it remains to be seen how they will survive in the long run, but I am very excited about how they are starting out.

The intention was that they would provide broad representation for their sectors to work with their government counterparts, to attack a variety of issues, many of which you have heard discussed here today.

I have to say, even as we were going through our formative process, we were already working with our government colleagues, doing, for example, detailed word-by-word reviews on the national infrastructure protection plan.

So we had that kind of interaction with them. The writing team that we have formed and which Paul co-chairs for us, that is working on the sector-specific plan, is made up of both industry and government representatives. So I am very positive on that.

Is there room for progress? Yes. I am very concerned that we need to quickly move on to reaching out across the country to the many different, some very key players who need to become aware of the sector coordinating council and become involved in it, as well.

When I spoke to the recommendation of encouragement and looking to our government colleagues, both the executive branch and Congress, for that kind of encouragement, you can do some of that when you are back in your districts and you are talking to executives.

You can build some of that encouragement, where appropriate, into legislation, where there might be an opportunity. I would like to see more of the senior executives in both the executive branch and Congress sending letters to the senior executives in the private sector, saying, "Look, this is an important activity. It will ultimately bring value to your company, help provide general protection to you, protect you in the mission or business services that you offer to your clients, and it will help the nation."

And even beyond that, because the whole issue of information security and cybersecurity is inextricably intertwined with many of our closest allies, but most particularly with our Canadian allies because of the border that we share and the way that our infrastructures happen to built and intertwined very, very closely.

So it is going to have international impact, as well, for them to participate.

I have watched with pleasure as some motivating factors have creeped into things that are extremely useful. So, for example, the federal financial institutions examination council has now built into their guidelines for examining information security and financial institutions a requirement that whoever provides their information technology and communications must be participating in an

ISAC, and that could be the company itself or it could be an outsourced company like mine that may provide those kind of services to them.

So that is positive reinforcement for joining those institutions and working together to solve these common problems.

Mr. LUNGREN. Thank you.

Mr. Barron?

Mr. BARRON. Thank you, Mr. Chairman. I think the sector coordinating council concept is working very well.

Telecommunications and communications, in general, has a longstanding history with the government through the national communications system and the NCC. We have been partners with them for well over 20 years and there is a close relationship there.

It has performed very well, 9/11, Katrina, I mean, we have been there and we have had a lot of success in the face of disasters. So I think that relationship and that partnership is, without question, there through the NCS.

The key is, I think, trying to turn the sector-specific plans from something that you are required to do to something that you want to do and we are making progress there and bringing in what I call, Mr. Chairman, nontraditional players into the Communications Sector Coordinating Council, cable telephony, those kind of folks who haven't traditionally been involved, but they are very critical players, are now getting engaged and we are very pleased with that, and think the NCS and the DHS folks are helping us with that.

So I think the partnership is working.

Mr. LUNGREN. Thank you very much.

The gentleman from Washington is recognized.

Mr. DICKS. Thank you.

Mr. Kurtz, when did you serve on the White House staff?

Mr. KURTZ. I joined the White House staff in 1999, before the millennium, at the very end of the Clinton administration and stayed on into early 2004 in the Bush administration.

Mr. DICKS. Are there people at the White House doing the kind of work today that you were doing at that time?

Mr. KURTZ. Not on a full-time basis.

Mr. DICKS. Part-time?

Mr. KURTZ. Yes. Certainly, there are people there within the National Security Council, Homeland Security Council and the Office of Technology and Policy who are spending some time on this issue.

Mr. DICKS. You described a little bit the—but flesh out why you think this has been downplayed in this administration. Why are they not taking this as seriously as the previous administration did? Obviously, you had the millennium, the 2000 thing, which was a big factor and had everybody's attention on it.

Mr. KURTZ. My own personal view is the Clinton administration, toward the end of the Clinton administration, they were, in fact, paying attention to this, because that is when we started to see the problems surface. The massive denial of service attacks in 2000 prompted an event with the president.

However, President Bush, when he first started off, one of the first briefings he took was on cybersecurity. When I was on staff there, it was one of the very first briefings he had and he stood up the critical infrastructure protection board, which, in turn, produced the national strategy to secure cybersecurity in 2003.

I think after that strategy was issued, that is when we had the change. Under the strategy, the vast majority of the work was to go over to the Department of Homeland Security. I believe that decision made good sense, because we were standing up the department at that time.

However, the department had massive issues on its hands and in my written testimony we talk about the preoccupation, and understandable preoccupation with the physical threats, threats to kill people, blow up buildings. That is understandable.

However, several years down the line, it is hard to defend that and especially in the context that we have increased threats and increased vulnerabilities and more dependency on this information infrastructure.

I also think the intervening events for the department have been, obviously, Hurricane Katrina. Katrina took a lot of energy out of the department. Really, though, quite frankly, I am out of excuses. The time is now to have higher level attention within the federal government to this issue.

And I would argue, and I talked about this a little bit this morning, that DHS needs to assert more leadership, but I would also argue that the White House needs to step up more.

Mr. DICKS. When you say leadership, what do you mean by that? When I look at it, either you are talking about resources, as an appropriator, or you are talking about regulation or you are talking about bringing together people to work together to try to understand each other's problems and to convince each of these sectors that they have got to do something themselves to protect their own cybersecurity.

Mr. KURTZ. I would argue, in a sense, all four of those issues that you mentioned, with the caveat around the third one, regulation.

By leadership, I mean—

Mr. DICKS. I know you are afraid of regulation, because of your clients.

Mr. KURTZ. But leadership, I mean—

Mr. DICKS. If you don't get the job done, and this goes back all the way back to the first days of the ICC and railroads. I mean, you know, at some point, the government has to step in and say you have got to do it.

Mr. KURTZ. But by leadership, I mean a senior individual who is consistently focused on a problem. One of the reasons why we have the national strategy to secure cyberspace, and I still think it has good standing in the private sector, is we had a very senior individual push that through.

Mr. LUNGREN. How about an assistant secretary for cybersecurity and telecommunications?

Mr. KURTZ. I think it certainly helps, but I do argue that we need to have more senior involvement on a regular basis by others within the department and other agencies, as well.

I think as far as resources, yes, resources, though, follow leadership when you can establish the priorities and programs that we need to pursue. Regulation in a limited degree, when we know we have had market failure, and there is an opportunity before the

Congress now to pass legislation to secure sensitive personal information.

There are multiple bills under consideration up here and I do think that is an important step forward that ought to be paid attention to.

Mr. DICKS. Privacy, obviously, is a very important issue. But, again, you think maybe having somebody else at the White House staff who is on the National Security Council and Homeland Security Council.

Mr. KURTZ. The decision to move it over to the Department of Homeland Security was correct and stands true today.

Mr. DICKS. But it was correct that they picked up the ball and did something with it, but so far they haven't done that.

Mr. KURTZ. Let me give a practical example. As we develop the IT sector-specific plan, we have been working very closely with our colleagues on a working level at the Department of Homeland Security. In fact, we have quite a good relationship.

But what is absent is that we don't have other agencies at a more senior level participating and only within the last week or so have we gotten people at the White House to, if you will, tune in more to this problem.

The reason why, I think, is that there are some very complex policy questions that need to be resolved that cross jurisdictions, that cross agencies. An example, in Hurricane, Katrina, ultimately, the president turned to the Department of Defense to help us in the response to Hurricane Katrina.

If we have a massive disruption in the information infrastructure, DHS is going to play a lead coordinating role, but you can be darn sure that DOD is going to care and the FCC is going to care. And what would happen in that instance is you would have probably not a total Internet blackout, but you would probably have very limited bandwidth available, which means information going across the Internet would need to be prioritized.

All right, so who is first? Does DOD take precedence? Does the financial community take precedence? Obviously, in the context of a larger scale disaster, first responders, hospitals, medical institutions, we haven't come close to making those decisions.

That is why I argue that we have to have more senior level input into this process. An assistant secretary can certainly help queue up those issues for more senior people to ultimately make those decisions. That is where the assistant secretary is critical, as he or she can work across federal agencies to queue up these decisions.

Mr. DICKS. Thank you, Mr. Chairman.

Mr. LUNGREN. The time of the gentleman has expired.

And the gentleman from Indiana is recognized for 5 minutes.

Mr. SOUDER. I thought that was a very interesting discussion, because we keep hearing leadership without specifics. But you put a finger on that it is cross-jurisdictional, because, in effect, if the secretary of homeland security and the Department of Defense are in an argument, what kind of official, short of the president or vice president, is going to be able to referee that.

There isn't going to be a national security advisor or a lower level staff and you have got, arguably, the two biggest agencies in jurisdictional tussles.

Let me come back to a variation of the question I asked earlier, and the answer was there is government enforcement and there is private sector enforcement and insurance was mentioned.

I was kind of trying to make a list in my head. What would be the government incentives to fix this? And, basically, other than altruism and a desire to help the American system, which is important and I am not arguing isn't a motivation, but it basically comes down to fear of loss of your job and career ruining.

In the private sector, the incentives are somewhat different. Has there been any court case that has established a liability of, if you haven't plugged a certain hole on cybersecurity, that you can have a massive fee on your firm?

Mr. KURTZ. The most obvious example that comes to my mind is the FTC, the Federal Trade Commission's actions over the past year and a half, where, in three cases, there were three retailers, separate events—well, two retailers and a data broker who did not take adequate steps to secure sensitive personal information.

Those entities involved knew that they had problems and didn't attend to them. And in one case in particular, the FTC levied a $14 million fine.

There have been subsequent cases and I think all of them have been less than $14 million. That is a relatively new development.

Mr. SOUDER. Because that will certainly affect insurance rates on everyone and the question is how to fairly disburse that, then, because your weakest links are going to be driving up the insurance rates on those who are actually investing, because the catastrophic costs drive up costs.

You also have potential loss of sales to any company that basically gets penetrated, because people say this isn't a safe place, or a financial institution. If it is others, you have the potential restoring costs to that, which the federal government would have, too, if we had damages in a facility that we run.

We also have the absolute wiping out of a brand name, in the sense of your company could be destroyed. There are multiple private sector things.

Why do you think, with all those pressures on the private sector, that the private sector, particularly given these kind of cases, isn't ramping up at a faster rate?

At the federal government, we react to problems. We need to be better at preempting. Certainly, Katrina and 9/11, voters want to know that they have every single bag—I mean, in this committee we debate this—want to have every single bag checked multiples times and this and that we put so much money in there that we are not dealing with cybersecurity.

We have X amount of money. That is risk assessment, ramping up, and the general public is reacting off of what happened in the past, to ramp up that and we are missing some bigger risks.

Part of my question would be, as the private sector, clearly, has multiple risks here, why aren't they ramping up more? Is it that the guys at the margin who aren't making as much money and don't have the ability to do the costs are the ones not ramping up?

Mr. KURTZ. I think that that last point is an important point. I think there are elements in the private sector, as I said earlier, that are taking this issue seriously, because if they experience a loss, it has a real impact on their business, their customers, their market share.

Mr. SOUDER. Can I ask you? Because my time is about—let me ask you, then. Given the assumption that you are saying, that if you have the ability, you understand the risk and you are doing it.

If it is the group—if our weakest link destroys our biggest link, in other words, you get into our electrical grid, whether it is in Canada or the United States, you are wrecked. If the weakest link, unless we have these firewalls that shut you off you are going to wreck everybody else around you.

If the financial market incentive isn't there for our weakest link, do we have a choice, other than the regulatory side?

Mr. KURTZ. I think, first of all, we need to pursue those incentives. I don't think we are at the point yet where we can say that the market has failed for all those industries who haven't necessarily taken it seriously.

Mr. SOUDER. Are there tax incentive type things that we could do to accelerate that?

Mr. KURTZ. I am certainly not going to say no to the idea of a tax incentive. I think we ought to explore that. But I think the insurance market is something interesting, because the reason why the insurance community, as I understand it, the reason why the insurance community cannot write as much insurance in this space as they would like is that there are, if you will, no common standards that they can base risk upon.

In other words, if I know X firm has done the following 10 things, that I have a reasonable understanding that a lot of other firms are going to follow, as well, and I can have that certified in some manner, self-certification or third-party certification, then I am going to feel, as a insurance person, and I have no background in this area, though, I would feel, as an insurance person, it is a better risk. I could write insurance in that area.

The problem is we don't really have that nexus now in the federal government between places like the Department of Commerce and the Department of Homeland Security to look at these issues.

If I can, the fascinating detail, I think, is currently, despite our dependence upon the information infrastructure, we have no federal agency today that is tracking the costs of cyber attacks. We have no one at the Department of Commerce, no one who is, if you will—we have all sorts of statistics as to how well our economy is doing, how our labor force is doing, how productive we are.

But when it comes down to understanding the costs of cyber attacks, the cost of disruptions, and, granted, it is a difficult problem to solve, no one is tracking that today.

Mr. SOUDER. Mr. Chairman, I would like to say, too, that in the GAO testimony, some of these things are out there, but they are usually way back in the reports or they do not put this clearly, but there is information in here about the slammer worm taking a nuclear power plant down, their security monitoring system, for 5 hours.

Somebody did a movie on that. I mean, our whole nuclear policy is based on that Jane Fonda movie. One movie and all of a sudden cybersecurity changes. Similar, that in here about?

Mr. LUNGREN. Are you suggesting Hollywood can make cybersecurity sexy?

Mr. SOUDER. Yes. And TV, in other words, when you look at the—if you are airline flights are canceled, your automatic teller machine failed, and network outages, if people knew what actually happened, it is scary.

And part of the problem, the way we respond is that, hey, we run every 2 years, the Constitution made us basically weather vanes and somebody has got to be blowing the weather.

And part of the problem we have in homeland security is we are charging around that way and cybersecurity has to become—the danger has to become more sexy to the general public.

Mr. LUNGREN. I thank the gentleman for his comments.

And now I would recognize someone who I would never call a weather vane, the gentlelady from Houston.

Ms. JACKSON-LEE. I will take that in the spirit that it is offered and I will wonder about the spirit.

Mr. KURTZ. He meant it as a compliment, I think.

Mr. LUNGREN. I meant an independent thinker is what I meant.

Ms. JACKSON-LEE. I said I would take it as such.

I am going to go with Mr. Souder's passion and continue at his level, which is where I stopped off, which is this sense of urgency that is not gripping some of the segments of homeland security as I think it deserves.

And so I am going to go back to you, Mr. Kurtz, and then Mr. Pelgrin, because as we look at the tragedy of terrorist acts, we know that Washington is certainly a target, but so are our notable areas of high risk, from New York to California.

And, of course, I happen to be a high risk proponent, but I do believe it is important to translate information so that all of the homeland can be secure.

But I have a simple question on time. You have laid out the obstacles, Mr. Kurtz, and Undersecretary Mr. Foresman, in a February 2006 press conference on cybersecurity or Cyberstorm, about the role of the department in the event of an attack, at the time, he said, "The key thing that you bring to the table is coordination. We will bring the ability to leverage multiple people towards a common goal, towards a common solution, in order to deal with the problem so that it is not a haphazard approach."

Well meaning, but the question is if you had to give an answer when the American people could feel comfortable that our cybersecurity is—the term under control is not accurate, but under extreme or very vibrant oversight, and our infrastructure is in lace and we have leveraged, when do you think that would be?

Mr. PELGRIN. I guess my response, from a DHS perspective, when we have an early warning system in place, a solid early warning system program in place that embraces the private sector.

Secondly, an emergency communications system that allows us to communicate when the very infrastructure we are seeking to protect is under attack.

Ms. JACKSON-LEE. Would you want that emergency system to be seamless, meaning that it would go across the nation, as opposed to saying all of New York would talk to each other?

Mr. KURTZ. Among critical owners and operators across the nation. In other words, key government entities, key folks within the private sector.

And then the third key area would be recovery and reconstitution issues. In other words, you have to accept that you have to plan as though there will be successful attacks. So what happens when that happens? How do you reconstitute the Internet? How do you reconstitute major protocols that may have been broken out there? We need to think through those.

Once we have those questions solved, we can accept that there are always going to be attacks. The nature of the beast is we are always going to have bad guys out there and always going to have people coming after us. But if we have a system in place to protect and respond, then we will be in a much better spot.

And, hopefully, along the way, we will have more resilient networks being developed through R&D.

Ms. JACKSON-LEE. Well, we think of Hurricane Katrina when we think of recovery. But for those of us who went to New York during 9/11 and went specifically to Wall Street, which was not hit, per se, but, obviously, was shut down, if, for example, an attack was on that system, the question is what is the timing of recovery.

What preparedness do we have? Because that system is obviously interwoven into the cybersecurity, if you will, superhighway, using an old term. And what is the recovery? I don't know if any of us know that.

Some of these things, I am sort of doubtful of discussing them publicly, but I think we have some real issues here and I guess I didn't hear a timeframe, but the fact that you have given me three elements would suggest that these three elements are not yet there.

Mr. KURTZ. No, they are not yet there. But in the case of the banking and finance industry, it is probably worthwhile for you to have a discussion with them, because they are very advanced in that area and they learned a lot from 9/11 and they have got some very sophisticated programs in place, which are worth learning about.

Ms. JACKSON-LEE. And the only question, I would say, is they are probably sophisticated, but are they complete and what more can they do and what more can we do to help them. I think that is the real question.

Mr. Pelgrin, the whole issue is to be able to communicate with state and local officials. Are we there yet, particularly on this aspect of security?

Mr. PELGRIN. I don't think we are there yet and it has to do a lot with still awareness and education and dollars and resources at the state and local government level.

I think we have made huge progress from when we started in 2003. The multi-state ISAC, we meet every month with all the states. We share information on an interactive call every month.

But trying to get that message out to local governments is a true challenge. We are working diligently on doing that and actually we have a pilot with five states, New York being one of those states, in which we are expanding the multi-state into local governments